Uncle Rob's Blog

More Short Bible Messages That Are Sure to Brighten Your Day

Volume 2

Rob Perkins

ONE STONE
BIBLICAL RESOURCES

Published by:
One Stone Press
Lovers Lane
Bowling Green, KY 42103

Printed in the United States of America

ISBN 13: 978-1-94-142297-7

ONE STONE
BIBLICAL RESOURCES

To my parents Bob and Geviene Perkins.
I don't know who or where I would be without them.

Foreword

Life is hard for teenagers. Biologically they are far farther along in life than the complexity of our post-modern society can allow them to be. Good parents are tasked with guiding their youths towards their understanding of a fulfilling life, while preventing irreparable social, economic, and spiritual harm. The fireworks between the youth that 'knows' they are an adult and demands to have the agency of one and the parent that knows better can leave marks on a relationship that last a long time. But even at this point, I argue, deep down teens know that their parents are not idiots. Someday in the future, they cannot quite admit to themselves, things will seem different than they seem today. The conflict is probably heightened when your dad is an Elder in the church to whom other adults go to for advice regularly. Or a doctor. Or a blogger with an international readership. These marks of legitimacy are burrs under the saddle to the wild stallion of youth. Still, deep down while shouting at the top of my teenaged lungs, I knew that some day my dad wouldn't seem so stupid.

What I did not suspect is that someday he would ask me to write the foreword to his *second* book. Teenagers, it turns out, can *never* know it *all*.

Contained in these pages are what I like to think of as folk wisdom. Folk wisdom has declined precipitously in the United States since industrialization. Partly because our communities aren't robust enough to generate it. Partly because preindustrial cautionary tales seem too quaint to 21st Century digital natives. That's where my dad—Uncle Rob—steps in. The stories, anecdotes, and parables contained herein are true, but more importantly they *contain* truth. Frequently that truth was not apparent to the person or persons that lived their event originally. Somewhere along the line Uncle Rob intersected with their story and did a lot of thinking on a tractor. Or on a boat. Or while my mom was trying to tell him something very important. That is to say that each page of this book has been purchased with real struggle by the subjects and real work by the author in order to get some truth into your hands. Sometimes that subject was me and my sister, or my mom, or people in our community, or folks at church.

Because there is truth in these pages, you'll laugh, you'll tear up, and you might just figure a few things out about yourself. I know I do.

—Walker Perkins
September 2024

Preface

When I became an Elder in our local congregation in 1997 I got all of the email addresses for our members and started sending out news about the congregation and a Bible based article every week as a means to enhance communication and build a closer congregation through the sharing of knowledge. That email list has grown to 250 recipients and includes members, former members, family and anyone who has shown an interest in reading what I write.

In 2009 my daughter encouraged me to start a blog (parkwaychurchnews.blogspot.com) and publish my articles there.

Robert Harkrider encouraged me to publish select articles in a book. Volume one was published in November of 2021 and at that time had 800 articles and 83,000 views. At the time of this writing the Blog has about 900 articles and 160,000 views.

When Volume one was published my daughter encouraged me to have a website (unclerobsblog.com). Both the Blog and the Website have the same articles.

The top three all time views come from the USA (74K), Singapore (44K) and Hong Kong (16K). I had no idea my writings would be so popular and far reaching. All I did was start writing and sharing with the congregation. Several have told me that they forward what I send out and of course the Blog is working 24 hours a day.

I owe a big thanks to James Rogers for doing the editing and to Marc Hinds for doing the formatting. Also a big thanks to Andy Alexander and One Stone Press for doing the publishing.

I hope you enjoy Uncle Rob's Blog Volume 2.

—Rob Perkins
September 2024

Contents

Lessons from Peter: Sink or Walk on Water

Matthew records the episode of Jesus walking on the water. Peter sees Jesus walking on the water... and I love this about Peter... he asks Jesus if he can walk on the water, too. Imagine Peter's excitement when he can walk on the water just like Jesus! But then Peter looks down, takes his eyes off of Jesus, gets a little scared, and starts sinking. Of course, Jesus won't let him drown.

In my opinion, this story foreshadows Peter's denial of Jesus. The Jews come for Jesus, and Peter sees Judas betray Jesus and all of the disciples, but Peter is still walking on the water and full of courage, so he pulls his sword out and attempts to defend Jesus. However, there are a lot more of the Jews than the disciples, and they have torches, swords, and spears, so Peter's faith begins to sink, and he runs like a scared cat.

Peter's fear turns to selfish protection as he denies Jesus three times (and takes his eyes off of Jesus) and he sinks even further into the water.

But wait! Jesus has already given Peter a life preserver and he has it in his back pocket. Jesus has warned Peter that Satan will tempt him, and he will fail. Jesus instructed Peter that, after his failure, he should swim back to the surface and get about the work of establishing the church.

We, too, may, from time to time, take our eyes off of Jesus and sink into the deep waters of sin, but remember Jesus is watching from Heaven and praying for us, and has his eyes on us watching to see if we will remember the great sacrifice he made for us, wanting us to swim to the surface and start walking on water again with him.

Beautiful Homes and Beautiful Lives

Julie and I built our home about 25 years ago. We contracted it ourselves and did a lot of the work ourselves (painting, finish carpentry, floors, etc.) We did a lot of the work ourselves because we couldn't afford the things we liked unless we did the work ourselves (we were poor).

Over the years, we have accumulated antiques and other nice things that suit our tastes. We still visit antique shops, but we only occasionally buy things if we think the items are worthy of replacing what we already have.

Consider 2 Timothy 2:20–21…

> In a large house there are articles not only of silver and gold but also of wood and clay…. If a man removes the wood and clay items [from his life] he will be an instrument for noble purposes, made holy, useful to the master and prepared to do any good work.

Of course, the author is using the figure of furnishing a house (by replacing things of lesser worth with things of greater worth) to furnishing a life with things of great worth to God.

Specifically, if there are things in your life like "evil desires of youth," "engaging in stupid arguments" and "quarreling" those things need to be replaced with "kindness to everyone" and "not being a resentful person" and "gentle instruction."

I'm sure there are a host of other examples of things that need to be replaced, but these are specifically mentioned in the text.

But look here… the purpose behind replacing these things is so that one can be made "useful to the master." For a young evangelist like Timothy, it would be so that he could lead folks to a knowledge of truth so that they will come to their senses and escape the trap that Satan has set for them.

Julie and I have furnished our home with things that we like because it brings us great pleasure, especially when guests come into our home who appreciate the same things that we like.

Julie and I attend a lot of estate sales and see all the accumulations of things that people have made being distributed and sold off. The other day at an estate sale, Julie told me that it made her sad, because one day that would be us… and she's right about that.

It's OK to have a nicely furnished home, but it is so much better to have a nicely furnished life because with that life you are useful to the Lord and on earth folks can look at you and say things like… look, there goes a real Christian.

And as we walk through the pearly gates of Heaven, angels will be waiting to shake your hand and say… we've been looking for you… well done, faithful servant!

Identify those ugly things in your life and replace them with beautiful things… you won't be sorry.

Forty Years and Forty Days

I was reading in Luke 4 the other day about Jesus fasting and being tempted in the wilderness for 40 days.

At the first temptation by the Devil of Jesus, Jesus quotes Deuteronomy 8:3, "Man shall not live by bread alone." The casual reader of the Bible might miss what the Jewish reader of the day must have seen very clearly. Jesus was referencing the 40-year wandering of the Jewish people in the wilderness. The fuller quotation goes like this...

> "You shall remember all the way which the LORD your God has led you in the wilderness these forty years, that He might humble you, testing you, to know what was in your heart, whether you would keep His commandments or not. And He humbled you and let you be hungry, and fed you with manna which you did not know, nor did your fathers know, that He might make you understand that man does not live by bread alone, but man lives by everything that proceeds out of the mouth of the LORD" (Deuteronomy 8:2–3).

Let's look at some similarities between what Jesus was doing and what the Israelites had done.

Jesus was baptized prior to the 40 days in the wilderness.

Israel was baptized prior to the 40 years of wandering in the wilderness (1 Corinthians 10:2).

Jesus ate nothing during his 40-day fast (God sustained him).

Israel ate nothing during their 40-year fast except for the manna which God provided.

Jesus was full of the Holy Spirit (which he received at his baptism) and was led in the Spirit into the wilderness.

Israel was led into the wilderness by God after Israel was baptized into Moses in the cloud and in the sea (1 Corinthians 10).

The 40-year wandering by Israel in the wilderness was a punishment by God for believing the bad report of the spies they sent into the Promised Land. In Deuteronomy, we find that its purpose was not strictly punishment but was also to humble them and test them, to see whether they would keep his commandments, and to teach them that their priority was not to serve their physical appetites (with bread), but to live by everything that proceeds out of the mouth of the Lord.

So, what does this say about Jesus' purpose in his 40-day fast and temptation?

Let me suggest that his 40-day fast was similar to his baptism . . . . It was to fulfill all righteousness. He wasn't baptized because he needed his sins washed away, and he didn't endure the temptation because it was possible for him to sin.

His 40-day fasting and temptation by the devil was to demonstrate his humility, to demonstrate passing the test of temptation and to demonstrate that he didn't live by bread alone but by following God. When Israel after 40 years humbled themselves and passed their test they could move on into the Promised Land.

The message for Christians today is that we also are undergoing testing, and passing that test starts with humbling ourselves and living by everything that proceeds out of the mouth of our Lord. And if we do that, we can join Jesus in our promised land.

Interacting with Kids

On the subject of child rearing, adults (other than parents) can have a major impact on the development of children. It seems to me that a lot of adults treat kids as if they are either non-existent or minor irritants. Better to be ignored than interacted with.

I love kids, I like joking around with them, picking on them and throwing the football with them after church. It is no coincidence that kids like me. Some have said that "Rob is just a big kid." OK, I'll take that.

I had a client in the other day who mentioned to me that her adult son commented that his time cleaning cages at Tejas with Walker were some of the most memorable that he had experienced. Interesting.... I'm sure Walker doesn't feel that way.

When Lauren was little, I took her on a farm call and pulled a calf. The rancher named the calf, "Lauren," she's never forgotten that.

When clients bring their kids into the clinic, I always shake their hands and introduce myself to them and ask them things like; "What did you get for Christmas?", "are you ready for school?", "what are you going to be for Halloween?", etc.

I ask them to help me lift their dog up on the table. There's nothing funnier than a five-year-old kid trying to pick up an 80-pound dog. Before I vaccinate their dogs, I give them a dog treat and tell them to reward their pet after I give the shots. I ask them if they want a shot or if they want their ears checked. If I have time, I take them back to the kennel and let them see all the animals.

I give kids empty syringes so they can practice being veterinarians at home.

Sometimes at church, I'll give things to the kids. I might buy a bunch of fossilized shark teeth on eBay and give them each a shark's tooth.

Brandon, my 9-year-old "little brother" in the Big Brother/Big Sister program, spends a lot of his time during the summer hanging out at the clinic with me. I've taught him to introduce himself, walk up to a client, look them in the eye, and shake their hands. Also, when they ask him how he's doing to respond in kind. Brandon can give a dog a shot and do lots of things around here.

Create some memories; teach these kids a thing or two… they will grow up one day.

Lesson from Sheep: Nutrition

The nutritionally wise Shepherd leads his flock to pastures that offer the very best nutrition. Sheep are herbivores, they are designed to eat grass, but can also browse on brush. In fact, sheep and goats are sometimes used to control brush in pastures.

In the show lamb business lambs are fed grain-based diets to develop the kind of body condition that will impress show judges. As a veterinarian, we see problems associated with feeding lambs a primarily grain-based diet. It is not uncommon to attend a sick lamb who has developed bladder stones and suffered a urethral obstruction that is potentially fatal. Sheep are not designed to eat grain-based diets and, as a consequence, suffer from various metabolic diseases (Chronic pancreatic inflammation, kidney disease, lameness and obesity).

Sheep love to eat corn, sorghum and all kinds of grains... it's like eating candy for them.

So too the church-flock.

Wise Shepherds feed their flock with a balanced diet of God's Word. Too many Shepherds and churches focus on things like...

Fighting the denominations. A bulk of teaching in these type of congregations focus on what's wrong with other churches.

Social things. Some churches minimize Bible teaching and focus on fun things... activities and eating and sports and the like.

Bible study. Some churches overwhelming focus is Bible study to the exclusion of anything social.

The positive aspects of God his love, grace, and care for his people to the exclusion of accountability and punishment.

The negative aspects of God, his hatred of sin and punishment and destruction to the exclusion of his mercy and forgiveness.

God's people need the right nutrition... a comprehensive balanced diet of God's Word and the social things that naturally follow that understanding.

An awful lot of teaching is soft and tastes good (like candy) but can lead to spiritually crippling and sometimes fatal spiritual disease.

Watch out for congregations whose sheep wander off and no one seems to care and whose sheep are spiritually weak and diseased.

If you want to be the right kind of Christian, look for a congregation whose Shepherds are wise and who care about their sheep and whose sheep are spiritually sound and happily flock together. The proof is in the pudding.

Crypt Horses and Wayward Members

Back when I was in large animal practice, one of the issues we had to deal with were "Crypt" horses. Those are male horses with hormone producing tissue in their abdominal cavity. "Crypt" horses behave like Stallions and are barely manageable.

The treatment is surgery, which has some risk involved. You can imagine laying down a 1,000-pound horse behind your clinic with less than perfect anesthesia and going in to find that hormone producing tissue. Clients usually ask if there is any risk involved. Yes, your horse might die. An old-time veterinarian told me he would tell clients ... "If he dies, you don't really have a horse anyway, do you?"

Often in congregations we have those members who wander away from our services. As Shepherds, we have the responsibility to try to herd those sheep back to the flock. Usually that means a phone call or two, sending a card or note, texting, messaging on Facebook, or trying to set up an appointment to go visit.

Many times, those things don't work. As a last resort, I try to just go knock on their door. Some people aren't comfortable with that and feel like it's an invasion of privacy, or it just goes too far.

I know this, that God is going to hold me personally responsible for the sheep in our flock, and I'd better have a good answer for Him when he asks me about what I did to take care of His sheep when I meet up with Him on the Judgment Day.

Those wayward members may never respond to any of our efforts, but let's try everything we can possibly do and if the "surgery" is a success, then it's worth whatever risk it took. Because after all ... we don't really have a horse anyhow, do we?

Medals and Humility

I read an obituary in the *Corpus Christi Caller-Times* last week. The subject of this particular obituary was a retired Lt. Col. from the army. He lived 92 years on this earth.

His children wrote the obituary for the old widower and mentioned that when they were cleaning out the garage, they came across a box that contained some medals... the Distinguished Flying Cross, Purple Heart, Silver Star and Bronze Star.

They were astonished... they had no idea. He had never mentioned any of those great honors. I think if I was one those kids I would have just sat there and cried. They don't just hand out those kinds of medals to just anyone. He had risked his life at great peril and shed his own blood probably to save his own men.

That, my friends, is great humility... to achieve so much and not ever mention it to anyone.

There's a great lesson to be learned by that in our spiritual warfare. Don't dwell on what you have done... how many people you have baptized, how popular you are as a preacher, how you defeated someone in a debate, how much money you gave to the poor, etc. Just keep working for God and don't even think about what you've done in the past and keep your good deeds a secret between you and God.

2 Corinthians 5:10 says we will give an accounting before the throne of Jesus Christ for both the good things and the bad things we have done.

I don't know what that venue is going to be like... if it's private or public, but if it were public and you were watching your mom or your dad kneeling before Jesus and Jesus just went on and on about the good things your parents had done... maybe things you never even knew about, wouldn't that make you proud? Wouldn't you just tremble at each word spoken?

I wish I had known Lt. Col. John W. Dean, retired. He must have been quite a man and if you ask me... deserved the Medal of Honor for humility.

Martha and Mary Have Jesus Over for Supper

When the two sister's brother Lazarus died, and Martha and Mary went to Jesus separately, one sister cried and caused Jesus to cry, and the other sister didn't. Martha and Mary were different and different is okay.

Which brings us to the story of Jesus eating a meal in their home, the text says that "Martha opened her home." Martha demonstrated hospitality to Jesus and his companions. I'm guessing that Martha's home was immaculate... everything in its place, clean and well swept. Not even a cobweb in the corner.

Jesus, of course, starts teaching and everyone there listens to him except... Martha. Why? Because Martha has invited the Master into her home, and she is worried and anxious about the details of being hospitable.

In fact, the text said, "She was distracted by all the preparations that had to be made." Things like setting the table, checking the food, making sure there weren't any flies in the house, things to wash feet with, etc.

Later in the text Jesus tells her... "You are worried and upset about many things..."

Martha couldn't listen to Jesus because she was "worried," "upset" and "distracted" and none of those things were sin-related. They were hospitality-related.

Here's another thing about Martha, not only was she not listening to Jesus, but she wasn't looking at him either... she was looking at her sister Mary.

Sometimes when we are worried, upset and distracted we take our eyes off of the better things of God and focus on what we think other people should be doing.

I'm sure Martha was surprised that Jesus was not more sympathetic towards her. She had presented her case to Jesus and asked Jesus to tell Mary to help her, but Jesus didn't. He told Martha in a gentle way that Martha was too worked up over relatively unimportant things and that Mary had chosen the more important thing.

I'm guessing that Martha sighed, took off her apron and sat down next to Mary and listened to what Jesus had to say and then afterwards they all got up and prepared the supper and enjoyed a meal together.

It's human nature to get worried, upset and distracted but an awful lot of it is caused by pressures we place upon ourselves and which we then vent upon others. Be careful about that and maybe take a long look at how we got there in the first place and just relax and listen to the Lord.

Martha, Mary, and Lazarus

John 11 contains the account of Jesus raising Lazarus from the dead.

Martha and Mary were at home with their brother when he fell sick. Everyone gets sick, but Lazarus day by day kept getting sicker. Jesus had been in the home of Martha and Mary at least once and probably several times, because he had developed a relationship with them. The scriptures said... he loved them.

Martha and Mary knew how busy Jesus was, but they feared for their brother's life and sent the message to Jesus..."Lord, the one you love is sick." A simple, understated message that hardly revealed the hidden emotions behind it... unless you were Jesus.

Even though Jesus loved this family, he waited two days to do anything about it. Imagine sitting at your brother's bed side as his health waned and viewing the agonized breathing that precedes death, and wondering why the one who could heal him hasn't come? I mean... you loved Jesus, and thought he loved you, and yet at the hour of your greatest need, Jesus doesn't show up.

Your brother dies, you bury him, and all the friends come to comfort you in your great sorrow... but Jesus isn't there.

Finally, the two sisters get word that Jesus is coming. Martha hears first and goes to meet Jesus on the road and says..."Lord, if you had been here, my brother would not have died." They have a brief conversation about the afterlife and, in spite of all the emotions and disappointment, Martha says..."I know that you are the Christ the Son of God who was to come into the world."

Amazing! In spite of Jesus' failure to help her brother she still believes.

Then comes Mary. She hears that Jesus is on the road and comes quickly. Maybe she even ran. Unlike Martha, when she sees Jesus, she drops to her knees and through her tears states the same thing that Martha had..."Lord, if you had been here, my brother would not have died."

Jesus sees her tears and is overwhelmed with emotion and cries himself.

Notice the difference in the two sisters and Jesus' response. Martha controlled her emotions and Jesus told her in a logical way the things she needed to hear.

Mary expressed her emotions and Jesus also gave her the thing that she needed the most... his emotions.

Jesus gave Martha the thing she needed to hear and gave Mary the thing she needed to see.

Of course, we know how the story ends. Jesus gave both sisters the thing they most wanted... their brother.

Just like Martha and Mary, we are all built a little different. One personality is not better or worse than the other personality.

We are all going to lose someone we cherish the most in the world. We may pray to God and their health may be restored, or we may lose that cherished person.

Remember Martha and Mary and don't ever lose your faith. Whether you have your loved one returned to you on earth or whether you see them in Heaven one day... God is in control and is the only one who can help you.

I like reading the logical things recorded in the scriptures, but I also like knowing that Jesus understands my emotions and can even read my heart when emotions overcome my logic and understanding fails me.

How Important is the Lord's Supper?

> His intent was that now, through the church, the manifold wisdom of God should be made known to the rulers and authorities in the heavenly realms, according to his eternal purpose that he accomplished in Christ Jesus our Lord (Ephesians 3:10–11).

When we consider the Lord's Supper, it's important to understand its purpose. When we understand its purpose, then questions like how it is observed and how often we take it can be answered easier.

Christians have assembly obligations... the Lord's Supper is one of those. Certainly, partaking of the bread and the wine reminds us of Jesus' body and blood and all the things represented by those things including the establishment of the new Covenant.

However, something else happens as suggested in the Ephesians text... God's wisdom is on display to heavenly/spiritual beings... demonic and angelic.

Think about this, as we are fulfilling our assembly obligations, including the Lord's Supper... Satan is furious, and God is happy.

When Christians decide to stay home and neglect the assembly and the Lord's Supper... Satan is smugly smiling, and God is sad.

Our assembly obligations have significance to ourselves, to our fellowman and to spiritual beings in the Heavens.

How often should we take the Lord's Supper? Apostolic example suggests weekly and that sounds pretty smart to me considering that every time we do... God's wisdom is on display.

At First You Caught My Eye

At first you caught my eye,
  And then you stole my heart.
I didn't think I could
  Love you more after that.
But now I realize
  You have even become
  A part of the person I am.
And my very finest qualities
  Come from loving you.

I saw these sentiments written on a card and I was struck by the profundity of their meaning.

The beginning of a relationship with all its expectations and in its naivete being satisfied with those early emotions and considering them to be complete and enough.

And then the progression to a more mature relationship and the surprise at what the "two becoming one flesh" really means. Things better understood by experience rather than the expression of mere words.

And then finally realizing that loving another person causes changes in our very own selves that we had no way of expecting. Changes that are awe inspiring. The transforming power of love.

What a blessing here on earth, but understand... the real blessing is being transformed into the very image of Jesus Christ. Becoming a part of him and realizing that our very finest qualities come from not only his loving us but also from our loving him.

That's hard to understand in the very earliest days of becoming a Christian and I suppose that's the way God meant for it to be so that we can wake up each day and reflect on where we've been, where we are, and where we are going.

Praise God!

The Tears of Jesus

Luke 19:41–44 tells of Jesus entering Jerusalem where he would be crucified in less than a week. As he entered, he started crying... not for himself but for the citizens of Jerusalem. As he entered, he saw children playing, mothers tending their children, old men sitting at the city gates, and people busily engaged with living their lives.

But Jesus saw something else, he saw about 40 years into the future and saw what the Roman soldiers would do to these very same people... besieging the city, starving the people, slaughtering the men, raping the women, bashing in the heads of the young children, and carrying the few survivors into captivity.

The prophetic vision of this horrible calamity caused Jesus to cry, but also caused him to want him to help them. His help started with offering faith to them. Faith that he was the son of God. To those who believed in him, he gave ample warning of when to get out of town and leave Jerusalem to save their lives.

He also sent his Apostles for 40 years after he died to work miracles and teach. The reality is that when the Roman soldiers surrounded Jerusalem to destroy it, the only people left in the city were those who totally rejected him.

God sent the Roman armies to punish Jerusalem and the Jewish system for crucifying his only Son. It was a well-deserved punishment, and yet Jesus, as he viewed the happy people of Jerusalem, cried for them.

I have to believe that as Jesus looks at us today, he still cries for those who are going to end up in the fires of Hell. Ample warning has been given and the punishment will be well-deserved, but he still sheds tears for those condemned souls... as should we.

Let's do the best we can to reach Heaven but let's also, like Jesus, care so much about others that we do whatever we can do to persuade them.

Lessons from Former Employees

Some will get mad for some reason and just walk off the job... no notice or anything. They put not only the business in a bind, but also their former fellow employees.

Some give notice and, especially if they have been a long-term employee, we'll give a card or a gift or buy lunch or have a going-away party and we wish them well, and mean it, too. We've had more than one employee leave but come back later because they missed the work, the camaraderie and everything we do. Sometimes the grass is not greener.

Like I say... I'm never very surprised at the way people leave except for what happened the other day.

We had a long-term employee who was one of our best who found a better opportunity, and we wished her well and did all the things we do for someone like that.

On the day that she left, she brought breakfast for everyone at work, and on the following Saturday night, she threw a party at her house for all her fellow employees. Wow... I've never seen the like. To my best knowledge, she isn't even a Christian... she was just raised right. Color me impressed.

There's a great lesson in that for Christians who may leave a job abruptly, call names, or write ugly Google reviews and the like. What kind of impression are you leaving? Would you be welcomed back? If they knew you were a Christian, would they like to come visit services?

Sometimes we all let our emotions get the best of us and do things we might later regret. There's a remedy for that... go and tell the person or former employer that you regret your actions and the things that you said. Maybe even bring them breakfast one day. I'm telling you that will get their attention, and God's attention, too.

The Trouble with Tithing

> "Be sure to set aside a tenth of all that your fields produce each year. Eat the tithe of your grain, new wine and olive oil, and the firstborn of your herds and flocks in the presence of the LORD your God at the place he will choose as a dwelling for his Name, so that you may learn to revere the LORD your God always.
>
> "But if that place is too distant and you have been blessed by the LORD your God and cannot carry your tithe (because the place where the LORD will choose to put his Name is so far away), then exchange your tithe for silver, and take the silver with you and go to the place the LORD your God will choose. Use the silver to buy whatever you like: cattle, sheep, wine or other fermented drink, or anything you wish. Then you and your household shall eat there in the presence of the LORD your God and rejoice" (Deuteronomy 14:22–26).

The above passage explains the Old Testament instruction of tithing. Of course, remember that Israelites were commanded to give back 1/10 of whatever their blessings were to the Lord. There was a problem though… they were to carry their 1/10 of grain, wine, oil, etc. to Jerusalem (for instance). That could be a potentially very long way to freight those products to Jerusalem and the Lord understood that, so He instructs them to sell it, take the money to Jerusalem, and use it to buy things worth their 1/10th tithing so they could fulfill the tithing commandment.

Of course, we're not required to tithe in the sense of Old Testament tithing today. Rather, we give free-will offerings… as we have prospered. So, it might be less than 1/10th and it might be greater than 1/10th. Some would say that since we live under a better covenant that it should be more than 10%

The Israelites had a problem giving due to distance. What kind of problems might we have today? I can think of two things off the top of my head.

We might "love" our money too much and have a hard time saying goodbye to it.

We might "love" things that money can buy too much and bought so many nice things on credit that our money is tied up and we can't give much to God.

Since we know that we have an obligation to give, and that God will hold us accountable, what kind of remedy might God suggest for our monetary problems?

God might say… don't live beyond your means. If you can't afford to pay cash for it, don't buy it.

God might say… why are you buying expensive things for yourself and giving me nothing?

God might say… it's better to live frugally and give bountifully than to live bountifully and give frugally.

I look back at my life and see that he has blessed me every step of the way. The reality is that if he asked me to give Him everything I have… how could I say no? Surely, Heaven is worth "all."

Score Your Marriage

Several years ago, some couples from church were going to get together to watch Gary Smalley's marriage enrichment tapes. It was the kind of thing where you watched the tapes and then had a group discussion with the intent to enrich your marriage. Julie told me about it and asked me if I wanted to go. I thought about it for a minute and said something like it would probably be a waste of our time since our marriage was in such good shape. Then she said, well we could probably help the others with our experiences. Ohhh… that woman is smart… really smart. So, simpleton that I am, I said, sure let's do it.

So, we started attending those meetings and, generally, they were good. I think I only fell asleep in one of them. But then we had one where Smalley said to rate your marriage from 1–10 (10 being the best) and discuss privately with each other what you individually could do to make your marriage a "10."

So, sure enough, Julie asks me on the way home how I rated our marriage. I was just about to say "10" when I thought, no, a ten is perfect, and she probably thinks our marriage is not quite perfect. So I was about to say "9" but stopped and thought no nine is like an "A"… I'll say "8" like a "B"… above average but still room to get better. So I told her "8." She said "8"!?!… I rated us a "6." I thought to myself, hmmph… a six… almost failing. So, then she asked me what I thought I could do to make our marriage better. I was well familiar with her complaints about me so I went through the list, blow by blow, of what I could do better.

Then, she asked me what I thought she could do better. I thought for a minute and told her that I didn't know anything that she could do better, and that I lied when I rated our marriage an "8," that I really thought it was a "10." I was perfectly happy with her.

It wasn't long after that that I noticed she was really treating me nice and I didn't really connect the dots. I just noticed how nice she was and thought well, we'll give it a few days and see what happens. But then the days turned into weeks, and I began to question her "is there something wrong with you?" Of course, she replied "no." Then I began to worry if the reason she was treating me so nice was that she was worried I was having an affair or something, so I kept asking her about it.

Finally, she told me that when I told her I was perfectly happy with her and didn't know of anything she could do better... that she knew I was wrong about that. So, she started with the premise that Smalley and others teach that you can't control anyone but yourself, so be the best you can and leave it to God and time to make your mate better and she worked hard to be the best wife she could be. So, I asked her well did it work... am I better? And that smart wife of mine said, "I can't really tell if you're any better but I'm happier this way."

Fertilizer and Fig Trees

> Then he told this parable: "A man had a fig tree growing in his vineyard, and he went to look for fruit on it but did not find any. So he said to the man who took care of the vineyard, 'For three years now I've been coming to look for fruit on this fig tree and haven't found any. Cut it down! Why should it use up the soil?' 'Sir,' the man replied, 'leave it alone for one more year, and I'll dig around it and fertilize it. If it bears fruit next year, fine! If not, then cut it down'" (Luke 13:6–9).

God has a vineyard and the Fig trees in this vineyard are people. God goes to inspect his vineyard and sees a Fig tree (people) that has not produced a single Fig in three years and so he instructs his gardener (Jesus Christ) to cut it down. The gardener (Jesus Christ) says let me fertilize the soil and let's give the tree one more year and if it still does not bear figs I will cut it down.

This particular vineyard is the Jewish nation. Under the old Mosaic Law they were not fruitful.

Jesus wants to infuse them with a new Law... a Law of love to see what they might produce. At the end of his three-year ministry Jesus allows himself to be sacrificed and gave up his perfect life to demonstrate incomprehensible love to his disciples. And with that love God's people who had been unproductive started sharing that love around the world and God's garden got bigger and bigger and produced more and more figs.

It's amazing what a little love can do.

Hospitality: Abraham, Lot and Sodom

In Genesis 18, we find Abraham cooling off during the heat of the day at the door of his tent. Three men approached. He ran and out to meet them and bowed before them and implored them to stay and visit. He washed their feet, he had Sarah (his wife) make cakes, he had a servant prepare a freshly killed calf and offered his guests, curds, milk and beef.

In Genesis 19, we find Lot sitting at the gates to the city. He sees two of the same three men. He didn't run to greet them like Abraham had done but he did bow down before them and invited them into his home. They entered his home, and he made them a feast and baked unleavened bread (not cakes) for them.

Further on in Genesis 19 we find the "hospitality" of Sodom. When the men found out the city had visitors, they tried to forcibly gang rape them.

What a huge extreme in hospitality between Abraham and the citizens of Sodom.

I suppose if you had to say... even though Lot demonstrated remarkable hospitality, Abraham illustrated the highest level of hospitality. The Sodomites were killed for their inhospitality.

How about today? What if some strangers approached you, what would your level of hospitality be? If you saw them coming from afar off, would you run and turn out all the lights and pretend not to be home? If they knocked on the door, would you say, this is not the best time? Would you think my house is a mess, and I have a headache, so come back another day please?

Sometimes we can plan hospitality and sometimes it's a spontaneous event... you don't get advanced notice. Have a hospitable heart and prepare for those events that come out of nowhere. God does test his people.

How to Hit a Home Run at a Funeral

Julie and I went to a funeral today for a member at church whose father just died. I didn't expect many of the members would be there because first off... no one knew the old man. But then also because this particular family doesn't attend very well and on top of that they just don't mix socially very well so I didn't figure many of our members would be there and turns out I was right about that.

Anyway, on the way there I told Julie that we were hitting a home run today and she said with who?

And I said with God. Then she commented that the reason she thought it was important to go was because of the way it made her feel when folks attended her dad's funeral.

Now I may be saying a little too much here but when Julie's dad died there weren't a great many people who attended his funeral and I think she was a little hurt by that, but she really appreciated those who did come to offer their condolences. So, you can see how important it was for her to attend this funeral for someone she didn't even know. By the way... she has a great heart.

Anyway, I know this about myself... I usually cry at funerals but I didn't think I would at this one because I only knew one person there... our member. But as I went to the front to offer my condolences to the wife and the other kids and their spouses... the tears started flowing (surprise, surprise, surprise) I apologized to them and explained that we knew the son and he attended church with us. When I got to the last person on the row (our member) we both cried and hugged each other.

I'm kind of reminded about that thing that Jesus said about not just inviting your friends to supper because you know they'll invite you back but how you should invite the folks that no one else is inviting.

That's kind of like funerals... don't just attend the funerals for your friends but attend the funerals of those whom you might not know so well. Everyone has feelings, don't they?

Who knows . . . you might just hit a home run with God or lift the spirits of one who is meek and gentle in spirit.

Marked for Death

I know a veterinarian who several years ago was called out late at night to see a colicking horse. After the exam the veterinarian determined that the horse was "twisted" and would either have to make the six-hour trip to College Station for surgery or would need to be put to sleep. The old man accepted the diagnosis, but surgery was not an option for him, and he was not really ready to put the old horse down. He wanted some time alone to say goodbye to his old friend and told the veterinarian he could do the euthanasia himself but didn't know where to put the bullet. The veterinarian got out a grease pencil used for marking cattle and put an "X" right between the horse's eyes.... Put it there.

There's a horse that had a sentence of death placed upon him and had the mark on his head to prove it. We all carry or have carried the mark of death on our heads as well. The scriptures tell us that whenever we break God's Law, he marks us for a death that will be carried out on the Judgment Day. There is only one way to have that mark removed, and that is by substituting someone else in place of ourselves. Fortunately, God has provided a substitute for us, and we can be spared that sentence of eternal death. However, the gift is a conditional gift, it requires us to quit breaking God's Laws and to live lives that mimic Jesus' life on earth.

The first consequence of sin is that we die and are punished eternally. Sin does something else to us. Sin steals meaningful lives from us here on earth. Sin shapes us into something ugly...righteousness shapes us into something beautiful. When we lie...we become liars and that takes away our trustworthiness. When we have sex outside the marriage relationship it ruins the beauty and trust of a committed relationship. When our priorities are wealth and pleasure our lives have no depth to them...we are behaving selfishly. Even if we live basically good lives here on earth, if we don't assemble with other Christians, we are neglecting our responsibilities to them and to God. God's Word does not teach solitary Christianity. The second consequence of sin is it ruins our lives on earth.

Don't allow yourselves to be shaped by sin and miss out on what this life has to offer and what God offers us in eternity. All those people not following Jesus Christ are like that old horse with an "X" on his forehead just waiting for the day when God places the bullet that condemns them to eternal punishment.

Scatter Shooting 2

When I was in the fourth grade (the first time), we lived in Utah. I guess Utah had a big grasshopper problem because mom gave us a jar of alcohol and paid us a penny for every 10 grasshoppers we caught. That's right, 10 cents for every 100. Every time I think about the three of us chasing grasshoppers all over the neighborhood, I want to call CPS. Never underestimate the power of a mother to manipulate her young charges.

When I was about 13, we had a litter of puppies. Mom said,"Robby don't you think you'd like to be a veterinarian one day?" I guess so mom. So, she kept reinforcing that idea until I thought it was my own. Now I wonder if I ever had any original thoughts or if they all came from my mother.

When I was in the seventh grade, I always wanted to arm wrestle mom, but she wouldn't do it because she didn't like getting beat. One day she wanted to paint my bedroom some sick color and I steadfastly refused. She asked me if she could paint my room if she beat me arm-wrestling? I said…sure, because she couldn't do it. So, she signed me up for life-saving lessons at the local pool. After swimming about 100 laps, I came home exhausted, and mom said…"do you want to arm wrestle?" Of course, I did, and she beat me. I looked at her grinning face and realized she had already painted my bedroom. Manipulative and cunning.

The last whipping I ever had was when I was 16. Actually, it was a mass whipping because mom ordered Scott, Greg and I to lay down on her bed and she proceeded to lay into us with a belt. I'm not sure of the offense but I am sure we were well deserving of the punishment. Anyway, we had learned to ignore the pain and just laughed instead. Pretty soon she started laughing and she never whipped us again. What a confusing scene that was.

When we would come to California to visit the relatives there were two big things we always wanted to do; go to the beach and go to Tijuana, Mexico. When we would go to Tijuana, we were always told two things. Don't buy any firecrackers and meet us back here at 4 P.M. What parents in their right mind left their three sons alone in a foreign country? I don't know but guess it worked out, except we always snuck firecrackers back into the states with us.

When we moved from Utah to Alabama, I repeated the fourth grade. Scott told Mom he was going to run away from home. Mom said… go ahead. Well, the little rascal did it. I still remember mom going crazy about it. So, while mom was searching all over Athens, Alabama for Scott, the police came by in a patrol car and told me to come with them. They had found Scott. So, when we picked him up, the cops told him that if he ever ran away again, they were going to throw him in the basement of the jail where they kept all the bad criminals (actually those were not the exact words). Needless to say, he never ran away again. I've always wondered if mom told those cops to say that.

Of course, we always had BB guns as kids and would try to shoot apples off of each other's heads and of course have BB gun wars. Uncle CB who was eight years older than me happened to shoot my cousin Sharron right in the buttocks and it left a horrible bruise. Of course, Sharron, destined to be a great mother one day, manipulated the situation by "over crying." So, here's what our parents did, they had Sharron lay on a bed with her naked bruised buttocks exposed but tastefully surrounded by towels and had us file in to see the damage. I still feel bad for Uncle CB about that.

Satan and Peter

In Luke 22:31, Jesus informed Peter that Satan had asked permission to tempt Peter and Jesus had granted permission. I wonder, why did Satan choose Peter? I think I know why.

Satan knows all the followers of Jesus, including you and I. Satan picked out Peter because he knew Peter was dangerous and important to Jesus.

Satan knew that Peter was the one in Matthew 16 who identified Jesus as the "Christ... the son of the Living God."

Satan knew that because of that confession, Jesus had granted Peter the honor of opening the doors to the Kingdom of Heaven by preaching the first Gospel message on the day of Pentecost.

Satan knew that Peter was one of three special disciples chosen by Jesus to witness his transfiguration.

Satan likes a challenge and always has. With God's permission, he personally tempted Job, one of God's best people. He tempted Jesus in the wilderness and finally he tempted one of Jesus' best soldiers... Peter.

Satan singles out God's best for temptation because the routine temptations of earthly living aren't enough to cause God's best to fail. Prepare yourselves to give your best to God and prepare yourselves to receive Satan's worst, and in so doing prepare yourselves for eternal blessings from God.

The Chicken Killer: Forgiveness and Restrictions

We have some family members who have a dog that I really like, and sometimes they will bring her to our house. One time though, when we thought she was in a secure area, she got out and killed one of our free ranging chickens. She was scolded and seemed sorrowful.

It wasn't a big deal (except to that chicken) because we still had 17 other chickens. I forgave that dog (although I do call her "Chicken Killer") and I still like her. But... I made a rule, whenever she was at our house, she had to stay on a cable or leash. We haven't lost another chicken since then, and I'm sure if the chickens could thank me, they would.

Sin and sinners are kind of like that dog. Yes, we can forgive them, even forgive them 70 times 7, but they need some restrictions.

For instance, the fellow who pilfers out of the church treasury. Yes, we accept his repentance, but he can no longer be involved in the church treasury... sorry... not sorry.

The guy involved in chronic, repetitive sexual sin. Forgiven? Yes, but perhaps no more unrestricted internet access to view pornography.

I'm sure there are plenty of other examples but those should suffice.

If all I did was forgive the "Chicken Killer" every time she killed a chicken, eventually I wouldn't have to forgive her anymore, because I would be out of chickens and we could be at peace, but that's a high price for peace.

Open your ears and listen to this... If we don't put restrictions on those who sin chronically and repetitively, we are complicit and guilty for those sins, and don't think the Lord doesn't know that.

Help the poor sinner to live a pure sin free life. You will be doing him, and yourself, a big favor.

True Beauty and Evangelism

There is a type of evangelism that is not accomplished through preaching or teaching, and that is evangelism that is accomplished through living the right kind of life.

1 Peter 3:1–6 teaches that concept. Husbands can be converted to Christ purely by observing the behavior of their wives. Obviously, Bible study enters in at some point, but I think the Apostle Peter is teaching that wives don't need to harangue their husbands constantly with Bible teaching, etc. but should just live their lives according to God's instructions and let God do the rest of the work.

Let's look at the text. First of all, wives need to be submissive to their husbands. That doesn't mean to never render an opinion or never to give advice but to respect her husband's headship in the family.

I've said before that many wives are smarter than their husbands. Many wives are more emotionally stable than their husbands and many wives make better decisions than their husbands. However, the really smart wife will not self-promote herself to her husband, but will, in humility, help her husband develop in his role of being head of the family.

Additionally, according to the text, a husband needs to observe purity and reverence in their wives. A husband may want his wife to engage in sexually improper activities. The pure wife respects her husband's headship but refuses to do anything that would stain her purity and ultimately stain her husband's purity because the two are... one flesh. What stains one also stains the other.

A wife needs to have a "gentle and quiet spirit." Especially when dealing with an angry husband, a "gentle and quiet spirit" is a great weapon. Too often when both parties become angry, the anger escalates, and improper things happen... words spoken that can never be forgotten and physical abuse. Whether you're a man or a woman, the smart person doesn't get sucked into a vicious cycle of anger that is only inspired by Satan.

The text says that a woman with a "gentle and quiet spirit" has a true beauty that never fades or diminishes... rather it grows and becomes more beautiful, and everyone can see it. Consider the opposite... a woman with a "contentious and angry spirit" just grows uglier and uglier.

Obviously, this type of evangelism doesn't have instant or quick results but is an investment in time and in God. This type of evangelism is practiced by men and women, and I suppose women are primarily being addressed here to give them hope and assurance.

God doesn't tell lies and this is a recipe that will work. Trust God.

A Few Thoughts on Healing in Luke 8

Here's a few thoughts on how Jesus heals in Luke 8.

The woman with a chronic bleed had been bleeding for 12 years so it was a regenerative anemia. Her bone marrow was producing enough new red blood cells to keep up at some level. I'm assuming that this was some sort of menstrual bleeding caused by a persistent estrogen producing ovarian follicle which would include other symptoms of menstruation like cramping.

So, she had persistent vaginal bleeding, cramping, and some level of anemia, which would have resulted in poor oxygenation of the tissues and chronic fatigue. I feel sorry for the poor woman.

When Jesus healed her, the blood flow was immediately stopped and, as she herself reports, she was immediately healed. That immediate healing could mean that all of her symptoms were gone... the blood flow, the cramping, the fatigue, and the anemia.

The 12-year-old girl was probably dealing with an acute problem, certainly not the chronicity of a 12-year condition. The list of conditions that young people suffer is a lot shorter than the list that old people suffer from. It was probably not organ failure, cardiovascular or cancer. She probably had an infectious problem. A lot of people then and now suffer from gastrointestinal infections and respiratory infections. Rapid dehydration from vomiting and diarrhea or lungs that are filling up with pus.

Whatever the problem was, she was at the "point of death." Usually, point of death looks like poor coloration to the tissues (purple not pink), coma, or agonal breathing. When I get a patient like that, there is usually not much that can be done. Whatever her final symptoms were, her Daddy knew he was about to lose her, and in an act of desperation, ran as fast as he could to find Jesus. His expectations were probably pretty low, but when you are about to lose the most precious thing in the world to you, you'll run after even the smallest chance.

When the family heard the news that she had died, they fell apart. They probably had a lot of questions like... Jehovah, we have devoted our whole life to you, how could you let this happen? Their friends were probably offering solace like… she's in a better place. Those are true words, but probably not enough to stop the flow of tears.

Jesus enters the room with just Peter, James, John, and the parents, and says don't cry she's just asleep. The text says they laughed at him. I imagine that their sad emotions turned to indignant emotions. Like… don't play games with us Jesus, we know what dead people look like.

Jesus takes their little princess and says "arise." She gets up immediately, and Jesus turns to her parents and says, "get her something to eat." Like everything's back to normal now. Go clean the house, mow the lawn, etc. Just another day for Jesus, but certainly not just another day for that family.

Their problem was that they really didn't understand who Jesus was, but that day they knew a little better.

Leadership from Nehemiah: Problems and Remedies

A long time ago, I heard an Elder say about another Elder…"He's the perfect government inspector; he identifies problems, but never does anything to solve them."

It's easy to identify a problem or to offer criticism. However, it is far more virtuous and beneficial to not only recognize a problem, but to take personal responsibility for the correction of the problem…like Nehemiah.

Consider Nehemiah, who was a Jew with an official position in the court of the Persian Empire which dominated the world at the time. He was the cupbearer for King Artaxerxes II and his queen. That meant he tasted the wine to make sure it wasn't poisoned. He was with King Artaxerxes every day.

Nehemiah had a great concern for his homeland, a homeland he had never seen. He made inquiry about Jerusalem and learned that the city walls were still broken down and the people were downcast and dejected. It troubled him deeply, and he spent four months in prayer about it and prepared himself for the opportunity to do something about it. When that opportunity came with King Artaxerxes, he identified the problem, offered a time frame for its completion, requested letters for travel and materials and got an armed escort.

Whether we have problems in the congregation, the home, or the workplace, don't make the mistake of being critical without offering well thought out remedies and personal involvement. The world is full of critics.

Lessons from Sheep: Defense!

In the Bible, God's people are often referred to as a flock of sheep and those in charge of God's sheep/church are called Shepherds or Pastors.

There are probably a lot of reasons for describing the church as a flock of sheep, but one very important reason is because sheep depend upon each other for defense.

Sheep don't have fangs or claws like a lion. They aren't swift enough to outrun a wolf. They can't spray repulsive scent like a skunk, and they can't camouflage themselves.

So, what can they do? In the wild they can group together in a solid circle with the rams and older animals on the periphery and the younger and weaker in the interior. A solid front can be intimidating to a predator, and the predator may skulk off waiting until an unsuspecting lamb wanders off from the protection of the group to acquire his prey.

Of course, domestically, a flock of sheep has a Shepherd who is constantly vigilant watching out for the flock... so too the church.

Just as flocks gather together to ward off predators, Christians congregate together and strengthen each other by learning about God, learning how to lead sin free lives, and by learning what it means to live a life of service until Faith is built up and fortified.

Once Faith is mature and the Soldier of Christ is fully armored, the great lion Satan will skulk away in fear. Especially if he is facing an army of Christian soldiers.

Remember what Jesus told Peter?

"Upon this rock I will build my church, and the gates of Hell shall not prevail against it."

There are a lot of reasons to congregate together with other Christians, and defense is one of those... even sheep know that.

The Parable of the Fat Guy

There was this fat guy who realized that he had become really obese, so he determined to join a gym and get in better shape. The next morning, he got up and ate a cookie and went to work and forgot all about losing weight. Later in life he developed type 2 diabetes, had to have one leg amputated and went blind from retinal microangiopathy.

There was another fat guy, he was determined to join a gym and get in better shape, and the next morning scheduled an appointment, joined the gym and went through his first workout. He got all out of breath and felt embarrassed at the way he looked and got really sore the next day and never went back. He too developed type 2 diabetes with all its complications.

There was a third fat guy. He joined the gym and started getting in better shape, but didn't do it consistently, and although he got in better shape eventually, he developed cardiovascular disease and lived the rest of his days in poor health.

There was a fourth fat guy. He joined the gym and consistently worked the program. While there, he made friends with more experienced members who gave him advice not only about exercise but also about nutrition. These friends were very encouraging, and he felt good about his new improved health and his new friendships. One day, he saw some fat guys coming into the gym and he was determined to help them just like others had helped him. He led a long, healthy and fulfilling life.

The meaning of the parable is this. The fat guy is a guy whose life is filled with sin. The gym is the church where God's word is taught and where Christians help each other to grow.

The first fat guy was determined to visit a church to get better but never did.

The second fat guy visited a church but didn't feel comfortable there, so he never went back.

The third fat guy joined a church but never really got involved... he was just there every once in a while. He learned some of God's Word but never really eliminated sin in his life and never got involved in helping others.

The fourth fat guy joined a church, loved the teachings from God's Word and allowed it to change his life. God gave him many blessings and he inherited a home in heaven for eternity.

Growing Avocados and Christians

I have failed at growing Avocados for many, many years, and that's not an easy thing for me to admit because I fancy myself as a bit of a horticulturist. I would buy an avocado tree which costs about $50… plant it, water it, and fertilize it. Invariably, in relatively short order, it would die, and I would be very frustrated and vow never to waste another $50 on an avocado tree. Eventually though, because I'm an optimist, I would try again with the same results.

Finally, I did some research and understood that Avocado trees grow up in a forest where they are shaded and protected and that tropical forests get consistent rainfall. You see we live in South Texas and those young trees were getting scalded by the sun and I couldn't water them as much as they liked.

So, I bought another avocado tree, and I planted it under some larger trees put it on a drip irrigation system. Voila! That tree is into its third year now.

Growing Christians… first of all, every human being in this world is a little bit different and some are a whole lot different. When they step out of the waters of baptism, they all have the same basic needs, like an avocado tree has basic needs… soil, water, and sunlight… but those needs have to be in the right proportions for that specific individual.

Every new Christian has to become grounded in God's word so they can know what God expects of them. In addition, every new Christian needs to build a social relationship with other Christians so they can learn from good examples. And they need these things in the right ways and in the right proportions.

You might lose a new Christian if you over/under fertilize or over/under water him. You might lose a new Christian if you set him out in the hot South Texas sun and don't have older more mature trees to protect him.

Christians like avocado trees need to be monitored on a regular basis… look for wilted and dropped leaves. You might think your irrigation system is working, only to find out that the batteries have failed.

You can't just hand a new Christian a Bible and tell him to attend every church service he can and figuratively pat him on the bottom and turn him loose. Care, protection, and monitoring must be given to every single individual Christian.

You can lose a $50 avocado tree from time to time, but woe be to the one who loses a new Christian due to laziness and neglect.

My Brother's Funeral

Well, I've missed two Sundays in a row at Parkway. Last Saturday night, my brother died unexpectedly, and we drove up to Bulverde to break the news to my mother. Yesterday, we had the funeral for my brother. I don't like to miss our services.

The funeral was well attended. It was standing room only and the attendance was estimated at about 230 or so. We had relatives come in from California, Tennessee, North Carolina, Oregon and from all over the state of Texas.

We had Christian friends from Houston that we had grown up with make the drive over. We had some of our Parkway family there, and some former members, like Linda Yanta and Doug and Paula Mokry. My old college friend, Ben Lucas, was there. A lot of these folks I hadn't seen since my dad's funeral in 1998. One of Scott's dentist friends made the trip from El Paso. He said Scott was so proud of his family and talked about us all the time and that he wanted to come meet us all. He also said Scott taught him a lot of dental techniques, and one time he was having trouble with a patient and called Scott, and Scott dropped everything to come and help him.

My emotions were in pretty good control until someone walked in that I didn't expect, or someone walked in who I hadn't seen in a long time. The Perkins family is pretty close, and one of my friends said they were a little jealous of that. Here's how close we are. Lauren had major surgery on Wednesday and still made it to the funeral on Saturday. She wouldn't have missed it for anything.

I made some opening remarks and had the closing prayer. My cousin Mark led us in "Amazing Grace," "I'll Fly Away" and "I Surrender All." Walker talked and all six of Scott's kids had something to say. I learned some things. My brother Greg did the eulogy. I begged off of doing anything because I knew I would break down emotionally, but I was assigned opening remarks and guess I did okay.

There were a lot of Church of Christ people there and the singing was awesome. A friend of my brother's widow was there and said she came to comfort Mary Jane but found herself being comforted instead and was amazed at the singing.

My friend, John Gambino, who has preached a lot of funerals said this... "The service today was the 'BEST' memorial I have ever attended. The candor, honesty, love expressed by so many was such a blessing. The understanding of and expressions of REDEMPTION struck a deep chord with me."

I'll tell just one story about Scott. He spent a week in jail one time, and he flourished in whatever environment he was in. When he was bailed out, all the other inmates stood up and gave him a standing ovation. That was my brother.

Our dad died in 1998 after a yearlong battle with cancer, and we had a year's time to shed tears and say goodbye. Four days before my brother died, I called him and sang happy birthday to him (66th birthday). The day he died, he was active in our Texas Perkins text message group. I wish that somehow, I could have talked to him just one more time and told him how much I loved him.

Citizenship

There is a big push in our country to limit immigration to this country, some of it so that immigrants will not compete with Americans for jobs.

I see a lot of hard-working immigrants in our country; Hispanics, Nigerians, Chinese… to name a few. I also see a lot of Americans who just flat won't work. They would rather live off of government programs.

If I had my way, citizenship in this country would not be based upon where you were born, but on your character and your drive to work. That's right… you could have your citizenship revoked based on a lack of these attributes.

That's not a strange or foreign concept. It describes something similar to what happened with God's nation, Israel. The people had become elitist and arrogant, and despised those who were not Jews. God condemned them for their lack of character… their hypocrisy, their inconsistency, and their twisting of his laws to suit themselves. He changed the rules for citizenship in his nation. No longer would it be based on who you were and where you were born… it would be based on Christian character… on faith.

Of course, basing citizenship in America on character will not ever happen and we are perhaps doomed to follow in the footsteps of Israel and become an "elitist, arrogant nation who despises those who are not us." Let's be good citizens of the nation of America, but more importantly let's be good citizens of the nation of God.

I Wish I Could Look into God's Heart

I was working in my garden today by myself, thinking about my brother Scott and his untimely death. I found myself thinking... I wish I knew a little more Bible, and I also wish I knew a little less Bible.

I am well familiar with passages like... "it's easier for a camel to pass through the eye of a needle..." and "strive to enter through the narrow door..."

But I'm also familiar with what Jesus did for the family of Lazarus, and how because of his great love for them, he made Lazarus alive again.

Now I know that making Lazarus alive again is not the same thing as living in eternity... I know that.

What I don't know is what my brother's eternal destination is. I worry that he didn't work hard enough to enter through the "narrow gate," but I also know that Jesus has great love.

I asked my mother that if we knew Scott wasn't going to Heaven would she offer to trade places with him? She didn't hesitate for half a second and said... of course, I would. And thinking about it, I guess I would too.

But if we were able to make that offer to Jehovah, God my guess is that God in his smartness would respond... let's see what Scott has to say about that. And, knowing my brother, he would reject that offer in a quarter of a second.

I wish I knew more Bible and wish I could look into God's heart, but if anything could get God to change his mind my guess is it would be love... ours and his. I guess we'll have to wait and see, but I believe in love.

Nicodemus and the Samaritan Woman

Two characters are introduced in John 3 and 4.

Nicodemus was a Ruler of the Jews, a Pharisee, and a Teacher of Israel. That means he was a student of God's word and knew it forwards and backwards, inside and out. He came to Jesus with a simple statement...

> "Rabbi, we know that you are a teacher sent from God because no one can do the signs you are doing unless God is with him" (John 3:2).

Jesus, never one to mince words or waste time, cuts to the chase.... "Except one be born again he cannot see the (coming) Kingdom of God" (John 3:3).

You see, Jesus knew who Nicodemus was and knew that Nicodemus knew what was in the Old Testament (from a human perspective). Nicodemus was obedient to the 10 commandments, kept the proper form of worship, kept the Sabbath and feast days properly, etc., etc., etc. Jesus just needed to correct some misconceptions that Nicodemus had about the coming Kingdom.

The second character introduced was different than Nicodemus. She was an unnamed Samaritan woman. In contrast to Nicodemus, she knew next to nothing about the Old Testament. As a Samaritan, all she had been taught and all she knew were the first 5 books of the Bible. Samaritans had improper worship and they didn't celebrate the Passover properly. The Jews despised them for their corruption of God's commandments.

Jesus was sitting at a well when the woman approached and asked her for a drink of water. The woman, knowing that Jesus was a Jew, was surprised that he would even acknowledge her presence and was bold enough to state that to him.

Jesus replied, if you knew who I am, you could have asked, and I would have given you living water. The conversation evolves into the age-old question between the Samaritans and the Jews... where is the proper place to worship? Jesus informs her that the Jews are worshipping correctly (and the Samaritans are not), but then proceeds to tell her that a time is coming... the coming of the Kingdom... when neither place will be the correct place to worship.

So, we might ask the question... why didn't Jesus answer the Samaritan woman like he did Nicodemus? Why didn't he tell her... "except one be born again he cannot enter the Kingdom of God?" And the answer is because they were in different places in their understanding of God's word.

The reality is Jesus taught them both the same basic thing. Both audiences had to believe that in the new Kingdom, citizens would have to worship in Spirit and in Truth. He just took different approaches to accomplish that task.

Of course, the same thing is true today. You cannot necessarily teach two individuals the exact same way, but we do have to end up in the same place. If we have the idea that we can just quote some passage like Acts 2:38 with the idea of accepting it or rejecting it and feel like we have done our job as a teacher, then we are sadly mistaken.

The Gospel is for all, including those who know their Bible (but misunderstand it) and for those who know next to nothing about the Bible. As a teacher, prepare yourself for every kind of student.

1 Corinthians 13: Love and Wedding Ceremonies

Most will recognize that 1 Corinthians 13 is the (so called) chapter on love. In fact, you don't even have to be a casual reader of the Bible to recognize the sentiments recorded there because these verses are often read at weddings and popularized in music.

I'm okay with reading these verses at weddings, but when done so they are a secondary application of these verses, and I'm not okay if our primary knowledge of Bible passages is based on a secondary application/understanding of said verses.

Note chapter 13 is found squarely in the middle of chapters 12 and 14.

Chapter 12 is about jealousy and envy among Christians in the Corinthian church about which gifts they had been given. Imagine that... God gives you something and you are envious of what God gave someone else. Sometimes, someone will complement me on some attribute or the other that I might have, and I'll respond... it's a gift and I can't take credit for a gift. Nor can you accept a gift from God and wish it were a better gift.

Chapter 14 is about the misuse of these gifts during the assembly of the church. Their assembly had become a chaotic assembly characterized by people interrupting and demanding attention for themselves.

So, Paul didn't take a break from talking about spiritual gifts to have a dialogue on love so that we could have nice weddings surrounded by the release of butterflies and white dove and a reading of 1 Corinthians 13.

Note in chapter 13 that Paul personalizes what he says... "If I (Paul) speak with the gift of the languages of foreigners and angels and have not love..." etc. etc. etc.

Things that love doesn't do... does not envy, does not elevate itself above others... etc. etc. etc. Things that love does... bears all things, believes all things, hopes all things... etc. etc. etc.

Paul is contrasting his behavior with their behavior especially as it is found in chapters 12 and 14 but really in the whole letter to the Corinthians. The Corinthians were childish, envious, jealous, tolerated sin, judged improperly, and some of them charged Paul with not being a true Apostle and therefore not worthy of monetary support.

Paul was striving for spiritual perfection, and if he suffered all that, he suffered and responded to their mistreatment of him in an unloving manner, then all was for naught.

Paul records the 13th chapter of 1 Corinthians to illustrate the stark contrast between his behavior which was characterized by actionable love and their behavior which was, in many ways, worse than the behavior of the pagans whom they lived among, and which bordered on blasphemy.

So, in summary I don't mind at all the secondary applications that are based on 1 Corinthians but as Bible students we're not worth our spiritual salt if we neglect or fail to understand the primary application.

Let's be salty.

Hophni and Phineas' Sins

There was a Priest in Israel named Eli, who had two adult sons who also served as Priests named Hophni and Phineas. Hophni and Phineas were doing some very bad things and their father Eli said this to them...

> "No, my sons; the report I hear spreading among the LORD's people is not good. If one person sins against another, God may mediate for the offender; but if anyone sins against the LORD, who will intercede for them?" (1 Samuel 2:24–25).

So just what were they doing that was bad? For one thing, they were having sex with some of the women who also served before the "Tent of Meeting," i.e. the sin of fornication.

The other thing they were doing was taking God's portion of meat that was sacrificed by the people of Israel.

So which sin was worse? They were both bad, but the sin of fornication could have been repented of, and sacrifices offered, and forgiveness given, but for the sin of stealing from God, there was no intercessor, and it could be punished by death.

In fact, isn't that the exact same thing that happened with Ananias and Sapphira? They made a verbal commitment to give a certain amount to God, but they stole part of it back for themselves and died for that great sin.

So, which sin was worse? Let me suggest that the sin with the greatest punishment is worse. Sinning directly against God is worse than sinning against another human being.

Which brings up the "unforgivable sin" that we read about...just what is that sin? Maybe it's sinning directly against God... the sin of Blasphemy.

Can we steal what is God's today and duplicate the sin of Hophni, Phineas, Ananias, and Sapphira? Probably. The bottom line is this... don't sin! Don't sin against other people, and certainly don't sin directly against God.

Both could have disastrous consequences, and one is worse than the other.

Satan: Such a Tool

Satan had it going pretty good up until about the time Jesus was baptized and received the Holy Spirit. Satan had plenty of Demons and they could live in anybody they wanted to with few restrictions. Satan had turned one of the 12 disciples (Judas), who would do whatever Satan wanted and Satan had received permission to test Peter, who failed the test and denied Jesus three times.

Satan did have a setback in his failure to induce Jesus to sin and his demons were starting to be exorcised. But he did have Judas in his pocket and was about to chop Peter's legs out from under him hoping to destroy him with depression and inaction after his failure.

Satan also was in control of the Chief Priest and the Jewish rulers and even though he hadn't been able to tempt Jesus he was going to have the son of God... killed. So, all-in-all, Satan must have been pretty happy with himself. Little did he know that he was playing right into God's hands and, in killing Jesus, allowed God to restore life to Jesus and hope to humanity and to limit Satan's powers and effectiveness by the giving of His Holy Spirit to those who believed.

Don't be afraid of Satan. We have God. Thank you, God, for what you did.

Sleeping Through Stormy Seas: Jonah and Jesus

There are two prophets identified in the scriptures who shared similar experiences… they were both in boats in stormy weather and were sleeping through the storm while the other occupants feared for their lives.

Jonah, in the Old Testament, had been sent to the Gentiles to deliver a message from God. He hated those Gentiles so much that he tried to outrun God, and God sent the furious storm… through which Jonah slept. He eventually repented and delivered (unwillingly) God's message to the Gentiles.

In the New Testament, Jesus and his disciples were crossing the Sea of Galilee when another furious storm struck. Jesus, of course, like Jonah, was sleeping through it. Unlike Jonah, at the behest of the disciples, Jesus spoke a few words and extinguished the storm.

And then, like Jonah, Jesus went to a Gentile country to do battle with Satan and cast demons out of a man and into a herd of unclean hogs.

Of course, Jesus was no ordinary Prophet… he was the Son of God and had the power to extinguish any kind of storm and carry his message of salvation to unclean Gentiles to make them clean and acceptable in the sight of God. And sent the unclean demons where they belonged… not in the temple of God but into unclean swine.

It can't be by accident that Jonah and Jesus both endured literal stormy weather, and I guess the message for us is clear… we can have great storms in our lives, usually caused by Satan, but with confidence and faith in Jesus Christ, those storms can be made calm so that we sail through life in calm seas and sunshine.

Give faith a try and let him lift you out of the storm.

Teaching the Creation on a Cruise Ship

On our recent cruise in the Baltic, I was talking to two of the crew members in the dining area. They were men in their early thirties and were in some sort of managerial position. One was from Romania and the other was from Serbia. I was entertaining them with a few jokes and was about to tell them my joke about how God created Eve. I always preface that joke by asking if they are familiar with the account of creation. I was dumbfounded when they said they were unfamiliar with how God created the world. Incredulous I persisted…you know, God created all the animals, he made the earth in six days?

They said they had never heard that story. I asked them if they were some kind of Muslim…they said no, they were Christians, but they didn't really read the Bible or attend church.

Incredible!!!

So, I got to teach the story of creation to two grown men on a cruise ship. I'm praying they start reading their Bibles.

Puzzles and the Bible

Sometimes, understanding the Bible can be like working a jigsaw puzzle. When you first start that puzzle, it's hard to get a clear and complete understanding of it. The more pieces you connect, the clearer it becomes and the easier it gets.

Growing up during the Christmas season, my mother would put a big puzzle out on the table, and we would work on it from time to time, all week long. It was a great family activity.

Usually, you do the corners and the straight edge pieces first... those are the easiest ones, but then it tends to get more complicated before it gets easier again.

I see my grandkids putting puzzles together, and sometimes they can force two pieces together that don't really belong.

Sometimes, when you're putting a big 10,000-piece puzzle together, it seems like an impossible task, and you just give up and walk away.

Sometimes, the cat knocks all the pieces off the table.

Of course, it always helps to look at the picture on the front of the box to help figure it out.

As the puzzle got more complete and there were just a few pieces left, we would race to see who would finish it first (sometimes we would hide a piece so we could put the last piece in).

Bible study can be kind of like working those old puzzles. It always helps to have a picture to understand where all the Bible pieces fit together. The picture that helps me is what Jesus said are the two greatest commands... to love God with all your heart... and your neighbor as yourself. If that's not what the final product looks like, then you haven't put the pieces together correctly.

Sometimes, people have a picture in mind (that isn't correct) and try to make all the pieces fit that picture. That's kind of like my grandkids forcing two pieces together that don't belong.

Some people try to minimize the Old Testament in the picture and make the picture all about the New Testament... big mistake... huge mistake.

Some people just think it's too complicated and give up too easily. Remember... it is just one book, and you have a lifetime to put it all together, and the more pieces you successfully put together, the easier it becomes. If it seems too hard, take a break and come back to it.

Understanding the Bible becomes easier when you have some friends to help you... just like a puzzle.

It builds community.

At home, when we would complete a puzzle, we would feel a real sense of accomplishment and leave it out for a few days just to look at it and remember the work we had put into it, but then we would take it apart, box it up and put it up in a closet where it never left.

That's the big difference between working out a puzzle and figuring out the Bible. Once we have that Bible figured out, it stays figured out in our hearts forever, and we can help the new Christian figure out how all the pieces fit together to get a true picture of God... and then rejoice together at the accomplishment.

The Parable of the Farmer

There was an old farmer who really knew how to farm. He could make a crop when no one else could. Part of it was that he was a hard worker. His wife was up and had breakfast made before daylight so he could get in the fields early. He usually had a big noon meal and took a nap right after but was back at it and worked while there was still light in the sky. He wasn't afraid of sweating or getting dirty.

The other part of his success was he knew his land. Oh, he had some land that anyone could make a crop on... the soil was deep and rich and low and caught the excess rain that ran off. Sometimes he liked to just go and watch it grow. The rest of his land was a bit more challenging; some of it was on a hill and didn't retain much moisture. On some of his land, the soil was thin and weak and if he didn't catch a rain at the right time his crops would dry up and blow away. On that land, if it got too dry, he would have to haul water to save the young plants until a rain came.

The other part of his land was next to a brush patch and tended to be a little weedy. If he didn't get out and hoe those rows four times during the growing season, the weeds would out compete his crop for moisture, nutrients and sunlight.

The old farmer was the right mix of hard work and understanding how crops grow.

In this parable, the savvy Farmer is an Evangelist, Elder, or any Christian who is interested in the souls of others. The crop in the weak soil is the new Christian who hasn't developed the deep tap root of faith... he needs a little help and protection until he can develop. The teacher devotes time and energy teaching about God and giving encouragement and support during stressful times that can be potentially overwhelming.

The crop in the weedy soil is the new Christian who has the wrong friends who pull him away from God and encourage a life of pleasure seeking. In this case, the teacher points out the destructiveness of that type of lifestyle and encourages other members to reach out and build relationships with this new Christian... replacing those old friends.

The crop in the deep, rich soil was just a joy to watch. These are the new Christians who don't need a lot of help. The love of God springs up in their heart and, with great energy, their faith grows in leaps and bounds. The teacher loves watching the power of God's word on deep and rich hearts.

Like the farmer, God's people can accomplish a lot through hard work and understanding, what it takes to protect a crop and get it to grow. No one ever said it was going to be easy.

The Court of Popular Opinion

1 Corinthians 5 contains a principle that, in my opinion, has application for us today, as well. Remember that the Apostle Paul was admonishing the Christians in Corinth for taking each other to court over legal matters.

Among other things, he advised them that their behavior did not reflect a good picture of the church to non-Christians.

Let me suggest that taking our problems to another court, the Court of Popular Opinion, might also reflect poorly on Christians and the church.

Nowadays, we have all kinds of platforms to complain about individuals and businesses... Google reviews, Yelp, Facebook, etc.

I personally have been called on social media both a "monster" and a "god." Which is the truth?

Probably neither. And here's the other thing on these types of platforms: you're only seeing one side of it because it does no good... no good at all... to start a battle of words on a social platform.

I've noticed on some social media arguments that people go back and edit their comments so that it appears that they didn't say at all what they did say, and the responder's comments then don't make any kind of sense. So, it's just better to stay out of those kinds of arguments.

I'm reminded of something my mother told me... if you can't say anything nice, then don't say anything at all.

Try to stay out of legal courts, and definitely don't take your issues to the Court of Popular Opinion. If you can't resolve your issue directly, then remember what the Apostle Paul said to the Corinthian Christians... it's okay to take wrong without complaint. After all, Jesus Christ is the supreme example of that, isn't he?

The Progressive Nature of Two Becoming One Flesh

Ephesians 5 speaks about a husband becoming "one flesh" with his wife. Husbands and wives become "one flesh" at the point of their marital union. However, there is a progressive oneness that develops in the relationship. That is... the quality of the oneness improves.

1 Corinthians 6:12–20 in speaking against casual sexual relationships between a man and a woman (or a prostitute) argues that improper sexual relationships corrupt the relationship we have with Christ by making us "one flesh" with a prostitute.

So, by definition, we can become "one flesh" with a woman merely by engaging in sex with her. The quality of that kind of oneness is minimal and transitory... even destructive. Certainly, the oneness of marriage cannot be compared to the oneness of a casual sexual relationship with a woman that we may barely know.

A husband and wife become one as they experience life's trials and joys together. Trust and confidence replace doubt and suspicion so that the relationship can grow. A seed is planted, and the young sapling grows into a sturdy tree that can withstand the perils of drought and wind.

The relationship is a progressive one and the two become "one flesh" as they live up to their marital responsibilities as outlined in the scriptures. Too often marital couples despair at the troubles they have and lack faith in God's transforming promise. Ephesians 5:32 calls it a great mystery and I suppose it is because it is better experienced than explained. Have faith in God and what he can do for you.

Pets and People

One of the things I see in my business is a very close emotional attachment to a pet. That's hard for some people to understand. However, when it comes time to put a beloved pet to "sleep," people frequently break down in tears and say that the emotions are so tough that they will never get another pet... they just can't stand to be hurt that way again.

I think I see something similar in people. They reach an age where they have lost their parents, their spouses, perhaps a child or two, and they just shut it down. The emotional investment is too tough, they seclude themselves, and they are just waiting to check out of this world and inherit eternal life.

In the dog and cat world, I always try to remind people about the joy they had with their pets when they were puppies and kittens, and all the things that made that relationship so precious. And how that relationship kept them from being... alone.

In the Christian world, we have a responsibility to live unselfish lives and to have an impact in the lives of others. An older person has a wealth of information gained from life's experiences that they can share with a younger person. It is our Christian responsibility to share that knowledge, and the relationship gained from that sharing... is precious.

I see a lot of funerals for older people, and the only ones in attendance are older people. I want to see some funerals for old people that are attended by a bunch of weeping and sobbing young people.

Pets are God's creation and his gift to us. Get a pet, but don't let that pet be a substitute for the affections that we should be sharing with others.

Build or Borrow

I bought an old Troy-Bilt tiller at the scrap metal yard the other day. The engine was locked up, but I only paid $50 for it. If I can get it running, I can sell it for $500. Harbor Freight has Chinese engines modeled after Honda's engines that can be purchased for around $100, and I considered buying one.

Instead, I decided to try to rebuild the old engine on my own. Buying a new one would be easier and quicker than rebuilding this old engine, but sometimes easier and quicker is not the best way to go. You can buy a new engine for $100, but you can't put a price on experience and what experience does for you.

Coming to know God's word is like choosing either to buy or build an engine. There are a lot of short cuts to gaining Bible knowledge. You can read commentaries and periodicals, or you can attend Bible classes and listen to preaching to get your Bible knowledge. Those things are easier and quicker than devoting yourself to in depth Bible study. The trouble with taking too many shortcuts is that we sometimes fail to develop our ability to think and analyze. We just borrow the opinions of others and make them our own.

We also ought to always restudy the doctrinal differences we have with denominations and restudy the issues that have divided churches of Christ and challenge our thinking.

I may end up buying that Chinese engine, but I'm going to do my best to get this old Briggs and Stratton going first, and whether I can or not... I'll be better for it. Study your Bibles first, and then read the opinions of men... you'll be better for it.

Starry's Pawn Shop

At lunch the other day, I drove out to Starry's pawn shop just west of Robstown on Highway 44. I like to go out there because Mr. Starry has a lot of stuff lying around that you can make good deals on. But I also like to go out there so I can visit with Mr. Starry. When you walk into his pawn shop, he's sitting in an easy chair pedaling some contraption to keep his legs in shape.

Mr. Starry is 86 years old, and I like talking to him because he's an old South Texas farm boy and he knows a lot of things. And he's colorful and I know how to talk to people like him.

He told me if he wanted to, he didn't have to work, and he could just stay home. I told him but Mr. Starry, if you did that, I couldn't visit with you. He stopped and looked at me square in the eyes and pointed at me and said that's it exactly. The old man likes to visit with people.

Then he told me a while back he was at Driscoll Children's Hospital, and there was a really sick baby and he and his wife decided to adopt the boy. He was 3 months old, weighed 5 pounds, and had what I would call divergent strabismus, but what Mr. Starry described as "looking at Georgia." He had ear problems, and he was born addicted to heroin. They fixed his eyes and ears and put him on Methadone. Mr. Starry said it took 7 months to cure him, and that every time the doctors reduced the methadone dose, the boy would cry for two days.

He told me the boy is in middle school now and doing fine. He told me they give the boy $5.00 for every "A" he makes, and one time he made four "A's," so Mr. Starry gave him $20. The boy looked at it and said... Dad, don't you think an 89 ought to be worth $5.00?

Anyway, Mr. Starry says that boy has added years to their lives... he comes home from school and fills their lives with joy and love.

I guess that's the way things are though.... The Lord told us not to think about ourselves, but to think about others. God bless Mr. Starry and his wife for helping someone who needed so much help.

It might do you some good to go see the old man every once in a while. It sure has done me good.

Planting Seed

I'm big into gardening. Sometimes, when I plant seed, it doesn't germinate. Sometimes, it doesn't germinate because I plant it too deep or too shallow or there is not enough moisture or too much moisture or the soil is not at the right temperature.

Sometimes, it's just bad seed. Good seed planted according to the directions will germinate and properly cared for it will grow and flourish. It is a fact of nature.

Another fact of nature is that God's Word is good seed. When it is planted in the proper conditions, it will grow and flourish. If we're planting God's seed and it does not grow, it's not a seed problem… it's a planting problem.

If we're planting rice in the Sahara Desert, we're probably not going to be successful growing rice. If we're planting God's seed in the hearts of people who care nothing about God's Word, we're going to have similar results. Jesus knew that. That's why he went to the discarded people of Jewish society, the prostitutes, the dishonest Tax Collectors, the unrighteous, etc.

He had some seed that when planted in their hearts could change their lives and who they were… and it did. I know how to plant tomato seeds. If they don't come up, it's a seed problem so I go buy new seed. If we're having problems with God's seed, we better reconsider how and where we are planting it… the problem is not with the seed.

Bad Sacrifices

> "It is you priests who show contempt for my name. But you ask, 'How have we shown contempt for your name?' By offering defiled food on my altar. "But you ask, 'How have we defiled you?' By saying that the Lord's Table is contemptible. When you offer blind animals for sacrifice, is that not wrong? When you sacrifice lame or diseased animals, is that not wrong?"

Malachi 1:6–8 demonstrates a principle of unacceptable sacrifice (or worship) to God. The Priests were not offering the best of their flocks for sacrifice but rather the worst. Oh yes, they were following the form of sacrifice, but the substance of the sacrifice was improper.

So, too, with sacrifice and worship today.

Prayer has been called the "sacrifice of our lips." Are our prayers more form or substance? Did we memorize a prayer when we were kids and still continue to offer that immature prayer to God on a regular basis, or do our prayers reflect spiritual maturity and spiritual excellence?

Do we celebrate the Lord's Supper in an obligatory way like making up our beds every morning, or do we look forward to it as a time of reflection and a time when we can come together as a spiritual family to demonstrate the unity of love to our Holy Father?

Do we unnecessarily substitute our assembling with watching services on TV? Isn't that a little like offering a one-eyed crippled lamb to God?

And in so many other areas.

As Christians, let's look at our flock and pick out the most excellent and very best lamb that we have to offer to God… he deserves no less and I'm not talking about sheep.

David Consumes Uriah

Most of us are familiar with the story that Nathan the Prophet spins to help David understand the severity of his sin.

In short, there was a rich man with many herds of sheep and a poor man with just one lamb. The rich man needed to prepare a meal for a visitor and took the poor man's only ewe lamb and killed it and prepared a meal for his guest.

Nathan asks David what should be done. David replies that the rich man deserved to die but should be punished by giving the poor man four of his lambs.

Nathan said... you are the man.

Remember that David committed two grievous sins... he committed adultery with Bathsheba and had her husband Uriah (one of the thirty mighty men) killed.

But wait, the story only points at one sin... adultery with Bathsheba not the murder of Uriah... or does it?

The rich man with many sheep is David (he did have several wives). The poor man with one ewe lamb is Uriah the Hittite and the ewe lamb is Bathsheba.

Let me suggest that the ewe lamb is a double figure. The ewe lamb not only represents Bathsheba and the addition of her to David's flock (of wives), but also represents Uriah, because in Nathan's tale, the ewe lamb is killed and eaten... and so was Uriah the Hittite, so David could have his wife.

Why didn't Nathan just confront David and say you killed Uriah and had sex with his wife? Because the illustration in a story helped David understand the enormous magnitude of his sin and God's enormous grace in forgiving him, and not punishing him with taking his life... which he roundly deserved.

David never forgot his sin and probably remembered it every time he looked into the eyes of his wife Bathsheba. We should remember it, too.

Don't Get Drunk

The letter to the Ephesians contains Paul's instructions to the Christians who lived in the city of Ephesus as to how to live their lives as Christians. Christians are supposed to live humble lives that serve others, and not proud lives that serves self.

> Be very careful, then, how you live—not as unwise but as wise, making the most of every opportunity, because the days are evil (Ephesians 5:15).

Christians must live their lives carefully and wisely consider the results of their actions.

"Do not get drunk on wine, which leads to debauchery" (Ephesians 5:18a). Debauchery means ... extreme indulgence in sensual pleasures.

Drunkenness is self-serving. It feeds our desire to have a good time and make idiots of ourselves. Drunkenness leads to sexual exploitation of ourselves and others. It is a destructive behavior.

> Instead, be filled with the Spirit, speaking to one another with psalms, hymns, and songs from the Spirit. Sing and make music from your heart to the Lord, always giving thanks to God the Father for everything, in the name of our Lord Jesus Christ submitting to one another out of reverence for Christ (Ephesians 5:18b–21).

Instead of being filled with alcohol, we should be filled with the Spirit of God, which leads to non-destructive behaviors ... behaviors that build others.

Being filled with the Spirit of God leads us to sing about God, to remember him, and build a spirit of thankfulness.

Be careful how you live, don't place yourself in an atmosphere of drunkenness. Surround yourself with spiritual people so you can be spiritual.

What is Wisdom?

1 Kings 3 records that God offered to give Solomon anything he wanted… anything. Solomon upon reflection asked for…

> "An understanding heart to judge your people, to discern between good and evil."

God responded…

> "Behold, I have done according to your words. Behold, I have given you a wise and discerning heart, so that there has been no one like you before you, nor shall one like you arise after you. I have also given you what you have not asked, both riches and honor, so that there will not be any among the kings like you all your days."

A description of the wisdom God gave to Solomon is recorded in 1 Kings 4…

> God gave Solomon wisdom and discernment and breadth of mind, like the sand that is on the seashore. Solomon's wisdom surpassed the wisdom of all the people of the east and all the wisdom of Egypt. He was wiser than all other people He also told three thousand proverbs, and his songs numbered 1,005. He told of trees, he told also of animals, birds, crawling things, and fish. People came from all the nations to hear the wisdom of Solomon.

I'm so glad that God gave the details of the wisdom, otherwise I might have thought he only gave Solomon an intimate knowledge of his written word… something that might be duplicated by the intense study of God's written word.

But no… Solomon was, among other things, a student and teacher of nature. He wrote down his wisdom in proverbs and was a great writer of songs, which means he was also a poet.

My guess is that Solomon was intellectually curious and had a thirst for knowledge… all kinds of knowledge.

Remember that outside of the Bible, God also reveals himself in nature so along with our Bible study... a study of nature and this world (God's creation) also teaches us about God.

If it is our desire to be wise, remember how God made Solomon wise and try to duplicate that path. And oh, by the way, through Solomon's wisdom he also became quite wealthy.

Proverbs 8:17–21...

> I (Wisdom) love those who love me, and those who seek me find me. With me are riches and honor, enduring wealth and prosperity.
>
> My fruit is better than fine gold; what I yield surpasses choice silver.
>
> I walk in the way of righteousness, along the paths of justice, bestowing a rich inheritance on those who love me and making their treasuries full.

Weevils and Sin

Most of those familiar with the cotton industry are also familiar with the Boll Weevil. The Boll Weevil is an insect that feeds on cotton bolls and can devastate a cotton crop. The Weevil entered the U.S. from Mexico about 1892 and by the year 1920 had devastated cotton crops all over the USA.

In fact, the Boll Weevils decimation of crops in the south was the primary reason for poor farmers leaving their lands and moving to northern cities.

Today, Boll Weevils have been eradicated in nearly all of the USA, and it happened in large part because of understanding the life cycle of the Boll Weevil.

There are three main elements in the eradication of the Boll Weevil...

- Plowing of the fields after harvest to reduce habitat for the weevil.
- Selective and planned herbicide use
- Reduction of Weevil populations by Pheromone baited traps.

The Boll Weevil kind of reminds me of sin in God's cotton field. Sin, uncontrolled and rampant, can ruin God's harvest of souls. What to do... oh what to do?

- First of all, God gave us Jesus Christ to save us from our own sins. His all-powerful blood is like the strongest of insecticides to totally eliminate the impact of sin in our lives.
- Then God identified the life cycle of sin, so we could see clearly how it occurs. James 1:14, "But each person is tempted when they are dragged away by their own evil desire and enticed. Then, after desire has conceived, it gives birth to sin; and sin, when it is full-grown, gives birth to death."
- And then God gave us the courage to conquer and eradicate sin. 1 Corinthians 10:13, "No temptation has overtaken you except

> what is common to mankind. And God is faithful; he will not let you be tempted beyond what you can bear. But when you are tempted, he will also provide a way out so that you can endure it."

I hope when God sends his harvesters and they come to our Parkway congregation that they step back and say...

"Whew... would you look at all that cotton. This congregation understood the seriousness of sin and the great price that was paid for it. They understood the pathogenesis of sin and had faith in God's promise that they didn't have to sin, and the results speak for themselves... boys, let's start picking... the master is going to be happy today."

Unexpected Phone Calls

Unexpected phone calls... we all get them. You're at work and you get a call... Your dad has cancer and has only 12 months to live. You're at work and you get a call... your wife has been in a bad car accident... come quick. You're sitting on the couch watching TV and get a call from Ray Torno... Linda just collapsed and died.

We moved here in 1982, and Ray and Linda were already members here. We don't miss services very often, and neither do they. So, for forty years we have seen them three times a week. When we moved here in 1982 and rented a house, Linda took her kids and went over and cleaned the place up for us before we moved in. She didn't even know us. So many little individual acts of kindnesses that when tallied together equal a heart bursting with love. We've attended all the funerals of dear and old friends with Ray and Linda. All the baby showers. All the wedding showers. All the picnics. All the social gatherings.

Linda taught our kids and grandkids. After class she would come up to us and brag on them and tell us how much she loved them and how special they were. She truly had a gift for teaching and rarely took a quarter off.

She and her work with the "kiddos" helped make Parkway special.

I was talking with Julie the other week and told her... you know... one of us is going to get sick and our health is going to fail and one of us is going to have to take care and to bury the other. It almost seems to me that the easier part is on the one whose health fails compared to the one who has to watch the person he loves the most in the world decline and fade away.

I told her... I hope you don't have to take care of me.

It's a time to mourn and reflect and we need this time. Linda is in a far, far better place, and my guess is that she'll find all the kiddos up there and love them with all her heart. Rest in peace Linda... we miss and love you.

Thank God we won't be getting any unexpected phone calls in Heaven.

Please pray and be there for my old friend, Ray Torno.

Esau and His Birthright

Most Bible students are familiar with the story of Esau. He was the oldest son of Isaac and Rebecca and as such was set to receive the "birth right" that his father (Isaac) had received from his father (Abraham). Of course, that "birth right" was the great promise made to Abraham that through him and his heirs, "all nations would be blest" (along with the other promises).

Esau, however, traded his "birth right" for a bowl of red stew. The scripture says he "despised his birth right." The Hebrew writer (12:16) describes Esau as godless. Let me suggest that Esau's despising of his "birth right" foreshadows the Jews despising of their "birth right" by their rejection of Jesus Christ.

Esau was so hungry for food (and didn't at the time truly understand the value of his "birth right") that he traded it off for a bowl of stew. He was godless and didn't believe in the promise of God.

The Jews were so hungry for their position of authority in their nation that they couldn't recognize the value of Jesus Christ and sacrificed him to maintain their position among the Jewish nation and the Roman Empire. They too were godless and didn't believe in the promises of God.

Later in life, Esau deeply regretted his hasty decision and begged his father with tears to receive the blessing of the "birth right," but it was too late. It was also too late for the ones who killed Jesus Christ.

The story of Esau also foreshadows events for us today. God still makes great promises to mankind. The wise will contemplate the great value of those promises and act accordingly. The foolish will reject them and chase after the pleasures in this life. What is it going to be... will we be wise or foolish? Learn the lesson of Esau. He is speaking to you and me.

Greetings and the "Holy Kiss"

Greet each other with a holy kiss (1 Corinthians 16:20).

This instruction is given five times in the New Testament and yet it is not something that is ordinarily seen among Christians today. Most say that it was a custom of the times, and the emphasis should be not on the "kiss" but on the greeting.

Christians are to greet each other... they are not to ignore each other. A greeting denotes a sense of worth. When we greet each other, we recognize even on a minimal basis that the other person exists. The warmth of the greeting is directly proportional to the sense of worth we feel for the person.

As an Elder, I position myself at the exit of the auditorium and try to shake hands with every person that I can. In preacher vernacular, that's "shaking them out."

Sometimes people complain that they don't know everyone. Solution? Stand shoulder to shoulder with me at the back door and you can get to know everyone.

A few years back, Julie and I were in Las Vegas for some continuing education. We visited at a church, and I remember thinking this church must get a lot of visitors. On the way out I shook hands with the Preacher and then decided I would help that church with their hospitality. So, I stood right next to the Preacher and shook hands and introduced myself to everyone in that building. Hospitality and greeting are not just the responsibility of the home congregation... visitors have a responsibility as well.

You know if Jesus Christ visited our assembly, I'll bet everyone would stand in line to shake his hand. Remember what he said, "... as often as you have done it to one of these you have done it to me."

I'm all for the Holy kiss... just tell me which you want (handshake/holy kiss) as you exit the building.

Lessons from Sheep: Value

In the Bible the Lord's people have been compared to a flock of sheep and their leaders are called Shepherds. God owns the flock, and the Shepherds are accountable to him.

One of the reasons for the comparison is because sheep have value and so do the Lord's people.

Sheep produce meat, dairy products, wool and Lanolin, etc. The Shepherd finds the best pastures for the sheep so that their nutritional needs are met, and they can be productive. He also protects them from predation.

The Shepherd may also vary the genetics of his flock by bringing in Rams who have the characteristics he desires (wool vs. meat types). Frequently a ewe may produce twins or even triplets. The Shepherd identifies sheep with superior genetics and maximizes their impact in the flock.

If a ewe doesn't produce a lamb every year she is culled as are the aged sheep. Every year the Shepherd gives an accounting to the flock owner.

The Lord's people/church has great value. Her Pastors/Shepherds nourish the flock by teaching from God's word. They are also taught to congregate/flock with each other. There is no culling of the aged in the church. The aged can still provide sound judgment and provide opportunities of service and honor for the rest of the congregation.

Those who possess superior spiritual genetics, if called upon, will sacrifice their own lives for the benefit of another.

The church's spiritual economic value is the good deeds she does for each other and for the community.

The goal of the Pastor/Shepherd is to deliver the entire flock/church to their owner (God) on the Day of Judgment… and that's exactly what God expects of them. Don't let God down.

Levi and Simon

The first recorded meal for Jesus and his disciples was recorded in Luke chapter 5. Jesus had just called Levi (publican) to be his disciple. Levi in his great joy prepared a great feast for Jesus and invited all his publican friends to eat with them.

Of course, publicans were despised by the Pharisees who would have nothing at all to do with them and probably accounted for Levi's great joy in being noticed by the great Prophet Jesus of Nazareth. My guess is that publicans loved collecting taxes from Pharisees and might even have overtaxed them in their glee.

Of course, when the Pharisees saw the great Jesus of Nazareth eating with the publicans they judged and criticized him (according to their standards) implying that a great Prophet would not associate with sinful and traitorous publicans (who probably loved to spend Pharisee gold.)

The second recorded meal in the Gospel of Luke recorded is in chapter 7 when Jesus was invited into the home of a Pharisee named Simon. A Pharisee was quite the opposite of a publican. Among other surprising things that happened was a woman who was a great sinner invited herself into Simon's home and attended to Jesus. Now Simon is associated with a sinner in his own home.

Perhaps she recognized that Simon wasn't much of a host and didn't afford Jesus with even a minimal level of hospitality... Simon didn't greet Jesus with the traditional kiss nor even supplied the basics necessities associated with cleaning his feet before a meal.

Simon despised the woman, and it would have never crossed his mind to invite her into his home. He didn't see anything in her... not even any potential for future righteousness. He was not moved by her tears or her or by any of her emotions. He couldn't see past her sin.

So why was Jesus' first meal with a publican (Levi) and his second meal with a Pharisee (Simon)?

Certainly, Jesus demonstrated non-biased hospitality by accepting the invitations of Levi and Simon... no matter their occupations or pseudo-religiosity.

Certainly, Levi was the better host. Undoubtably, he greeted Jesus with the customary kiss and afforded him with the necessities of foot washing (if not washing Jesus' feet himself).

Levi did not camp outside of Simon's house to look for an opportunity to critique Jesus... like why would Jesus associate with those who prayed on street corners, etc? He was too humble for that, and he had faith that Jesus could rise to any occasion.

Simon, however, was not humble, and maybe felt himself to be superior to Jesus. He may have even been one of the Pharisees who stood outside Levi's home criticizing Jesus.

I suppose one of the lessons of these two suppers was to illustrate what true hospitality looks like, and the honor that a hospitable person offers his guest... even a guest of the humblest station.

What would happen if we invited the preacher into our home and he brought a nasty homeless person with him? Would we shun the homeless guy, or wash his feet?

I think Jesus ate in the homes of a tax collector and a Pharisee to illustrate that he cared for all people, as so should we all.

A Miracle Interrupted

Luke 8 records a miracle interrupted by another miracle. Jesus is on his way to heal a 12-year-old girl who was about to die when a woman with a 12-year illness interrupts him.

The Ruler of the Synagogue approached Jesus on his knees to beg Jesus to cure his daughter. The woman who was slowly bleeding to death had no one to intercede for her and had spent every dime she had hoping for a cure. Unlike the Synagogue Ruler, she was "unclean" and stigmatized for her uncleanness.

For the Ruler, it was like the journey was taking forever... crowds of people thronging Jesus slowing down the travel time. And then Jesus stops and asks, "who touched me?" Another delay... everyone was touching Jesus. His daughter could die at any minute, even seconds could make a difference. If only he could get Jesus to his house so he could lay his hands on her and cure her before it was too late.

Finally, the woman comes forward and identifies herself. And then Jesus says something that was probably lost on the crowd but was not lost on the reader. He says, "daughter your faith has made you whole." You see there were two daughters in this story, one who was 12 years old and one who had been sick for 12 years. They were both important to Jesus. And just as he says those words the father hears some other words... your daughter has died.

One daughter healed and one daughter dead. In the mind of the crowd Jesus is batting .500, but what the crowd doesn't know is that the game isn't over for Jairus, and his little daughter and Jesus is still batting and when Jesus bats he hits a home run every time.

Sometimes someone dies and people think what a shame she was so young and beautiful, almost like if you are plain or ugly it's no great loss. The learning point for us is that Jesus cares for everyone whether she's a 12-year-old girl or someone who has a disease for 12 years that everyone including the doctors have given up on. Jesus doesn't give up on people he values and loves every single soul and so should we. Don't ever give up on anyone . . . just stay in the game and maybe, just maybe you'll jack one out of the park with Jesus' help.

Abraham and Abimilech

Abraham and his wife Sarah moved into the region of Gerar in which Abimelech was king when Abraham was about 100 years old, and Sarah was 90 years old.

Abraham judged the people of the area as having no respect for God and worried that they would kill him to possess Sarah. So, worried for his own life, he asked Sarah to present herself as his sister. Sarah was indeed his sister (and wife) as they both had the same father (different mothers).

Abimelech, King of Gerar, sees Sarah and is apparently smitten by her great beauty and takes her. In those days and times Kings had all kinds of power and could take any single woman they wanted.

God prevents King Abimelech from having sex with Sarah because he knows Abimelech has a clear conscious and doesn't want Abimelech to sin ignorantly. However, as punishment for this sin of ignorance, he prevents Abimelech's wives and concubines from conceiving. Abimelech is in total ignorance of any of this until God visits him in a dream.

In this dream God tells Abimelech he is "as good as dead" because he had taken a married woman with the intent to have sex with her (commit adultery). God also identifies Abraham as being a Prophet with the ability to pray for Abimelech to keep God from killing him (he has a way out).

The penitent Abimelech restores Sarah to Abraham. He tells Sarah, I am giving your "brother" 1,000 Shekels of silver to cover the offense.

Abraham prays to God for Abimelech and God "heals" him. Here are a few take aways...

God interacts in the affairs of mankind. He certainly did in this case, and I see nothing in the scriptures to show that he has stopped.

You can be punished for sins that you are ignorant of. Be careful with your actions, someone may be manipulating you, but you are still responsible to God for them.

The punishment can include a negative effect on the quality of your life and even death. If your life isn't very good right now, it may be due to some sin against God that he is punishing you for.

Abraham's faith had not fully matured (even though he was a prophet). He was still afraid of what others could do to him. Your faith may not be very strong right now but don't give up… it can get better.

Abraham was selfish, he was willing to sacrifice Sarah's honor to protect himself. That's pride… serving self and not others.

Abraham manipulated Sarah by asking her to do something wrong to demonstrate her love for him. A lot of men manipulate women by prefacing a request with "if you love me."

Sarah allowed herself to be manipulated and her weakness almost caused an innocent man to be killed.

Abraham mis-judged people, he told half-truths and concealed the other half, he manipulated his wife into a deception, and he lacked faith in God.

God still loved and cared for him.

I suppose God revealed all of Abraham's weaknesses as a message to you and me. God isn't looking to punish his faithful people when we occasionally make bad decisions. It's not a deal breaker for Him. What is a deal breaker is open rebellion against Him. When we make mistakes and sin, we should recognize it, repent, and strive to do better, and not despair and give up. Have confidence in God… he is our Father.

Picture This

Imagine with me if in a church someone had got busy and converted a bunch of Pakistanis to Christ and someone else had converted a group of bikers. And you walked in that church and all the Pakistanis were sitting separately together and all the bikers were sitting with each other... Anglos, Hispanics, etc.

What would you think about that? You might think that church was divided and segregated.

That's kind of what was happening in the church at Corinth. Some were trying to distinguish and differentiate themselves by who they were baptized by... Paul, Apollos, Cephas, Christ. In other words... I am superior to you because my baptizer is superior to your baptizer.

Paul said they were full of "jealousy and strife" and as such were failing as a church which according to God's plan was supposed to demonstrate love and unity to the world.

That sort of division could lead to a division of the church itself a la Acts 20:28–30, in which "grievous wolves" drew people away to start a new church. New churches such as the "Followers of Paul" church, etc.

It's nice to associate with other Christians who might have a similar culture (racially) or to associate with other Christians who have similar hobbies... such as riding Harley's, but we have to be careful how we present ourselves to the world because we might appear to be divided and not united.

As members of a congregation, let's develop relationships with all of our other members. Members who are racially different, old and young members, male and female, etc. so that we can demonstrate to the world the wisdom of God that, in spite all of our differences, we share the commonality of Jesus Christ which is life changing.

Let's be diligent and cautious about presenting the right picture to the world because you might only have one shot at it.

Reasons Why God Doesn't Answer Prayer

One of the reasons God doesn't answer prayer is because sometimes we pray for things that are under our own control. The scriptures say, "If a man won't work neither let him eat." Imagine this: there is a fellow who has the ability to work, but he won't, and instead he prays to God for food. God is not going to answer that prayer for food because the man has the ability to provide for himself. That's the easy one... how about these?

A husband prays for a stronger marriage with his wife but is unwilling to follow God's instructions to him as a husband. He's selfish, unloving, and doesn't care about the needs of his wife. He always places her second. Will God grant him a stronger marriage in spite of his rejection of God's Laws on marriage? Probably not.

A man goes to the doctor and is diagnosed with Congestive Heart Failure. The doctor tells him to lose 50 pounds, change his diet, and exercise more and sends him home with the appropriate medications.

The man prays for healing but does not follow the doctor's instructions. He goes to the cafeteria, orders a chicken fried steak slathered with cream gravy, has sides of mashed potatoes and macaroni and cheese, and ice cream for dessert. Then he sits down on the couch and watches TV. Will God answer his prayer for healing? Probably not.

There are several reasons God doesn't answer prayer. One of them is that God won't help us unless we're willing to help ourselves. Follow God's instructions and, if you still have needs, pray to God and prepare to be richly blessed.

The Eye of the Needle

In Luke 18, Jesus tells the very rich Ruler of the Jews to sell everything he had and give it to the poor and "follow me."

The rich ruler turned away in sorrow, and Jesus said these very famous and troubling words...

> "It is easier for a camel to go through the eye of a needle than for a rich man to enter into the kingdom of God" (Mark 10:25).

By definition, in the scriptures, the "poor" are identified as not having the daily necessities of life: food, clothing, and shelter. Therefore, compared to the poor, those who have those necessities are rich.

I personally do not know anyone who fits that definition of being poor. Everyone I know is rich.

You might develop the idea that it's best to be poor that God doesn't want us to be rich... not true.

The promises of the Mosaic Law were that those who obeyed it would be prosperous on earth.

In the Sermon on the Mount, Jesus said that those who put the kingdom first would have all the necessities that they needed in life.

In fact, when someone comes into the church building begging, I tell them that I know what their problem is... they haven't put God first.

So how are we going to get that camel through that needle?

1 Timothy 6:17–19 identifies several things rich Christians are to do.

- Be not high minded or arrogant
- Have hope set on God, not personal wealth
- Do good and be rich in good works
- Be ready to distribute or share their wealth
- Be sympathetic to the needs of others.

An example or two might be handy:

Zaccheus dedicated 50% of his paycheck to help the poor. If he wronged anyone financially, he not only returned their money. but gave them 4× back.

Righteous Job instructed many, steadied the weak, and braced up tired knees.

So how do we get that camel through the needle?

Easy... don't make it your goal in life to become wealthy. Our goal should be to serve God with the totality of our being, and if God wants us to be wealthy, he will make us wealthy.

The Lesson of the Spotted Sheep

In Genesis 30, Jacob was having a disagreement with his father-in-law Laban as to the division of their flocks.

Jacob proposed that he take all the sheep that were spotted, and Laban could have the more valuable pure white sheep. Laban readily agreed to that.

The trouble for Laban was that God blessed Jacob, and the majority of the lamb crop each year was spotted and Jacob's flock prospered while Laban's flock diminished.

Jesus during his three-year ministry consistently chose the spotted sheep to minister to… the prostitutes, the tax collectors, the hypocritical Pharisees, the sick, and the dying.

Of course, the Lord's church has been compared to a flock of sheep, complete with Shepherds (Elders) who care for the sheep. The Lord's church does its best work with spotted sheep that need shepherding.

Sometimes in a congregation we might want to "pick" our sheep. Oh, here's a nice moral family in a denomination let's clean up their misunderstandings about the Bible and add them to our number and we can go out and eat and be friends and laugh and have a good time.

But the best work is accomplished when we can find someone filthy with sin and show them a little light at the end of the tunnel, and with great patience and great spiritual stamina, stick with them through thick and through thin until they become strong enough to stand on their own two feet. That, my friends, is a great victory over Satan, and causes the angels in Heaven to rejoice.

And if there is anything to be learned from the Lesson of the Spotted Sheep, it's that God will make that flock of sheep great and prosperous to the bewilderment of folks like Laban who considered spotted sheep to be inferior.

And we're not talking about sheep and flocks but rather people and congregations.

The Prodigal (and Loved) Son

The Father:

I don't know where I went wrong with Caleb. Maybe I was too hard on him or maybe I was too soft… I just don't know. His mother Abigail died when he was just a toddler, and I just couldn't bring myself to remarry. Every time I looked at Caleb as he grew up, I could see more and more of his mother in him, and I don't know… it kind of hurt.

Seth wasn't anything like Caleb, he was big and strong, and I could count on him to do the work we needed on the farm… he loved farm life, and I loved him for loving what I loved.

Every time we went into town on the Sabbath, Caleb was always hanging around with kids his age who were a little on the wild side, and Caleb seemed to like to hang around the Gentile boys too.

I knew that, sooner or later, I was going to lose him, and then one day he came up to me and said… Dad, I'm of age, and since I'm not going to inherit this farm anyway, I just want my inheritance to try something different.

I didn't really trust what Caleb was telling me, but I knew if I didn't give him the money, he would resent it and I would probably never see him again. I watched him gather his things and watched him walk down that road until he disappeared. Oh, Jehovah God what have I done? Where is Abigail when I need her the most? Please protect Caleb for me!

The Prodigal Son:

I remember when I got that money from my Dad that I was finally going to do things my way. I was tired of Seth being the favorite son… Mr. Goody Two Shoes.

The Gentile boys had told me what life was like in Ammon… drinking and dancing and girls who knew how to do things that I couldn't even imagine. I had a great time for a while until the money began to run out. Once the money was gone, my drinking buddies were gone too.

The girls quit smiling at me and flirting with their eyes. I lost all my money, I lost all my friends, I lost a place to stay, and now I was stuck sleeping with these unclean hogs doing a job no one else wanted to do for pennies. I was always hungry and had nothing to eat but hog food.

Dad could never forgive me... I had slept with unclean gentile girls and now with unclean hogs. But maybe Dad would let me be a servant... they had beds to sleep in and ate three meals a day and lived happy lives.

I'll go back home and be a servant in my father's house. Every step I took on the way back home, I rehearsed what I would say... I'm sorry Dad, you were right, and I was wrong. You were so right that I am not even worthy to carry your name. Please let me be the least of all servants in your home.

The Father:

Ever since Caleb had left, the first thing I would do every morning when I got out of bed was get on my knees and pray to Jehovah God to bring mine and Abigail's son back. Then, in the afternoon, I would sit on the porch of the house and watch the road to see if my prayers were answered.

I knew right where Caleb was. I knew he was in Ammon, and I knew what he was doing there. I had heard that he had run out of money and was down on his luck.

I also knew that if I wanted him back forever, I couldn't go after him. He had to make up his own mind to come back.

One day, I was watching the road and I saw a solitary figure approaching. I didn't want to get my hopes up just to be dashed like had happened so many times before. But as the figure got closer and closer, something about him seemed familiar... the way he walked... the way he held himself. Could it be?

As he got closer and closer... it had to be Caleb... it had to him. I jumped up and ran to him. It was him! It was him! He started to say something about not being worthy, but I didn't let him finish... I couldn't. I hugged his neck and started crying, and then an amazing thing happened Caleb hugged my neck and started crying, too.

We held each other for a little while, and I realized all the servants were watching. I told them... get these filthy clothes off him, bathe him, and dress him like he deserves to be dressed... like my son... because Jehovah has done a great thing... he has returned my lost son.

The Older Brother:

A little later, Seth came in from the fields and, when he heard the news, he was angry and said, "Dad I have worked side by side with you all my life. Caleb wasted your money and disgraced our family name. How could you honor him this way when you have never even thrown a party for me?"

The Father:

"Seth, Seth . . . I've made a lot of mistakes in my life, but you are not one of them. You are everything to me. I couldn't do anything without you by my side, but Caleb is your brother and the second son of your own mother. Yes, he wasted the money, and yes, he behaved in a disgraceful way, but doesn't sorrow and repentance count for anything?

"Jehovah God brought your brother back, and unless I miss my guess, he'll be twice the brother and twice the son he was before."

If Jehovah can forgive, so can we and so should we.

Plenty: Food or Poverty

> He who tills his land will have plenty of food, but he who follows empty pursuits will have poverty in plenty (Proverbs 28:19).

Look at the way this proverb is put together. You can have either "plenty of food" or "plenty of poverty."

The Lord wants his people to be industrious. There are plenty of Proverbs that teach this. Having a good work ethic is something parents should teach their children. My dad was a great role model for me, but even now as an adult, I am still influenced by people who are hard workers.

I was talking to my brother, Greg, the other day, and he said when he was in high school, he had a job washing dishes at a restaurant. The manager called him over and said he wasn't working hard enough. Greg told him he was working harder than the other guys, and the manager responded, "don't pattern yourself after them." Greg said for the next month he worked as hard as he could, and the manager noticed and approached him, impressed with Greg's work ethic and offered him a job as a cook. Greg said, no . . . I quit. The manager was disappointed at losing a good worker.

Greg told me that our brother Scott gave him some advice one time. Scott told him that when the boss is away most people slow down, but that is when you should work twice as hard . . . not to impress the boss but to earn the respect of the other workers and to differentiate yourself from them.

People who are industrious and who take pride in their work ability will never go hungry, they will have plenty. And they will be noticed and rewarded for their skill.

Do you see a man skilled in his work? He will stand before kings; He will not stand before obscure men. Proverbs 22:29.

Two Greatest Blessings

In Ephesians 5, the relationship between Christ and the church is compared with the relationship between a husband and a wife.

Ephesians repeats what is stated in Genesis in regards to the husband and the wife. Namely, that the "two shall become one flesh." This relationship is revealed as a "great mystery." However, Ephesians states that this "mysterious" relationship also applies to Christ and his people.

In short, husbands and wives become one through a lifetime of sharing life's troubles and life's blessings. These experiences, when coupled with two people obeying God's commands, regarding marriage, result in two people having a deep appreciation for each other and a mate that is highly valued and regarded as irreplaceable.

Too often in the early years of a marriage, troubles seem insurmountable and the marriage, and its vows, are broken and the two remain two. In addition, even when the marriage remains intact, if God's laws regarding marital responsibilities are not followed, the two remain two. However, when the two overcome life's obstacles and respect God's laws, the two can become one. There is no greater physical blessing on earth.

Similarly, people often give up on Jesus Christ and the process that leads to oneness with him. They give up on the three hallmarks of Christianity; Bible study, living sin free lives, and lives of service to one another.

Just as there is no greater physical blessing than being one with a mate, there is no greater spiritual blessing than being one with Jesus Christ. Don't miss out on the two greatest blessing God has to offer. Pay the price to make it happen.

My Dad

I've been having dreams about my dad, that he didn't die and was still with us, but his illness had changed him . . . he was older and more feeble and he didn't talk much anymore.

In the dream I had last night, I was on a road trip with him, and he was driving, and we stopped at a gas station, and he went up to the cashier, and when he was backing up, he bumped into a woman, and he stumbled a few steps, and fell to the ground. I ran up to him crying and said . . . Dad . . . Dad, are you okay? And he looked up at me, and I helped him up, and I told the woman how sorry we were.

I really miss him, but I guess everyone who has lost their father also misses them.

Dad, of course, loved the Lord. When I was active on a Christian discussion list, he copied all my posts and kept them. I found them when I was going through his things when mom moved out of their home.

I've always written in my Bible and made notes and such in it, and we were home one weekend, and Dad happened to pick up my Bible and started looking at it. I'll never forget when he just kind of held that Bible to his heart and didn't say a word, but just kind of gave me a look that he told me he was proud of me.

I'm sure Dad told me he loved me, but I don't really remember him saying it, but I never doubted it because he showed me love in so many ways.

I also don't doubt that he's in Heaven and he's happy up there. I wonder if the Lord lets him know how his family is doing. If he does, then I know Dad is really happy.

I've wished that the Lord would let me have one day with him, so I could catch him up on some things like how well my son and daughter have married, and introduce him to my six grandchildren, each one of whom is so special to me. I would like to take him to church with me and introduce him to all the members who are also so special to me. And just let him know how much the Lord has blessed me.

I guess that will never happen, but I have a great hope and base my faith on the fact that Jesus was raised from the dead and I will be, too, so that I can catch up with Dad in eternity.

In a few years, my son and then my daughter will turn 44 years of age and when they do, I'll tell them (if I'm still alive) that they are the same age as when I lost my dad and let that sink in.

Anyway, I woke up this morning crying, remembering a dream and wishing I could see my dad just one more time.

The Lost Sheep, the Lost Coin, and the Lost Son

Luke 15 starts out by describing the reaction of the super-righteous Jews (Pharisees and Scribes) to Jesus' socializing with the worst sinners of Jewish society. They criticized Jesus and felt morally superior to him.

Jesus then tells three stories: the lost sheep, the lost coin, and the lost son. There's a progression in these stories.

A sheep wanders off, the shepherd leaves 99 sheep to go look for the one that was lost and when he finds it there is great rejoicing. Of course, everyone knows that.

A woman loses one of her 10 coins. She searches the house to find it, and when she does, she is overjoyed and tells her friends, and they rejoice. Of course, she does.

A man has a rebellious son (one of two sons), who leaves the family and goes to a far country and lives a live of debauchery and sexual misconduct. The son repents and comes home, and the father rejoices and throws a big party in celebration. Some understand this and some don't.

The super self-righteous Jews criticized Jesus for caring about the lost children of God. Their spirituality was messed up. They mistakenly thought that God's children couldn't have anything to do with those whose lives were sullied by sin.

Perhaps they thought those lost should repent first and clean their lives up, and then and only then could there be any social contact. Sound familiar?

They were spiritual failures. They didn't understand that God loves all his children and is anxiously awaiting the day that they would repent and that repentance always, 100% of the time results in great rejoicing in Heaven. Maybe, not always on earth, but always in Heaven.

They didn't understand the process of bringing people to repentance. They didn't understand the need for social contact to demonstrate care and concern and correction for the ultimate well-being of those who are lost in sin.

When I'm working with someone, I have to ignore a lot. I have to ignore bad language, bad behavior, bad jokes, immodesty, etc. So, I can build a relationship to show Christ living in me so that they will look at their own lives and want something better. If I condemn every little thing, I lose my chance to address the greater things.

I've seen that process work.

Jesus worked hard with the morally bankrupt of Jewish society... should we do less?

One Flesh with Christ

Ephesians 5:22–33 is a passage of scripture that compares the husband/wife relationship with the relationship between Christ and the Church. Usually, these passages are used to learn about the husband wife relationship, but clearly the import of these verses is to teach about Christ and the Church.

> For this cause shall a man leave his father and mother and cleave to his wife; and the two shall become one flesh. This is a great mystery: but I speak in regard of Christ and the Church.

So, how does Christ and the Church become one flesh?

Just as a man desires a wife that is pure and has not been in a physical relationship with another man, Christ desires that his "wife" be pure. Certainly, we are not pure when we come to Christ. We are soiled by our relationship with Satan who we follow when we sin. Christ, however, has made provision so that we can be pure and virginal, in regards to sin, when we enter into a relationship with him. His self-sacrifice, the giving of his blood, cleanses us of our sinful relationship with Satan and makes us pure… totally pure.

We enter our marital relationship with Christ when we arise out of the waters of baptism having our sins washed away. Then we are cleansed and truly a bride worthy of a relationship with Christ because he has made us pure and worthy.

A condition of our marital relationship with Christ is subjection. Christ requires that his bride live by his standards. If she does, the reward is great… becoming "one flesh" with Christ. Experience the mystery. There is only one path.

The One- and One-Half Talent Man

We're all familiar with the five-, two-, and one-talent men, but there is an implication in the text that there exists a one-and-one-half-talent man. He is the man who, instead of burying his money, like the one talent man, turned his money over to a bank so his master would at least receive interest.

I suppose this might be considered a minimal level of acceptability to the master but...probably not. Let's consider a few things.

The one-and-one-half-talent man did not have confidence in his own ability, so he shifted his responsibility to someone else. He feared his master.

The five- and two-talent men doubled their investments, which would be a 100% return. They worked hard to please their master. They loved the opportunity to please him.

At a bank, one would be lucky to get a 3% return. Probably not a return the master would be happy with.

If the master just wanted a 3% return, he could have put the money in the bank himself.

The one-and-one-half-talent man probably suffered a fate similar to that of the one talent man. They both feared their master.

God has high expectations for his people. He has made a considerable investment in us and blessed us with many blessings and abilities. He expects a high rate of return on his investment. Don't be afraid of God. Fear can be incapacitating and encumbering. Love God and believe in his love for you and you will be able to do many things.

There's a Fungus Among Us

Most people know that yeast is used in the manufacture of bread. There are many kinds of yeast, but the specific yeast that is used in the making of bread is "Saccharomyces cerevisiae," which means "Sugar-eating fungi."

The flour dough is kneaded together with the yeast, which eats the sugars in the dough and releases carbon dioxide, which makes our bread nice and fluffy. The process is called leavening. In Latin... "to raise."

In the scriptures, yeast is used figuratively to describe what sin does in a congregation (1 Corinthians 5) and how the Kingdom of Heaven changes the world (Luke 13:20).

In congregations, if sin is ignored and not addressed, it has the potential to affect the whole congregation and change the congregation described in its purity as unleavened bread to impure leavened bread... a fungus (sin) has entered and changed the congregation.

In the Parable of the Yeast (Luke 13), the world is like a lump of dough. God's word is like the yeast... it permeates and penetrates the dough (world) and, like a fungus, eats up all the sugars (sin) and changes the world to righteousness, which is tasty and delectable to God.

As Christians, we should be careful not to let the yeast of sin corrupt us and potentially corrupt the church.

If we do that, then the sinlessly pure collectivity of Christians (the Church) can spread like a fungus through the whole world and bring glory to God.

Put Your Armor On

Ephesians 6:10–20 concludes a section of the Ephesian letter that begins in Ephesians 4:1.

Ephesians 6:10–20 contains a well-known section of scripture that not only encourages a Christian to stand and be strong, but also tells the Christian how to do it... by putting on the whole armor of God. Not just some of the armor, but all of it.

Things like...

- loins girded with truth breastplate of righteousness
- footwear that is associated with the gospel of peace the shield of faith
- the helmet of salvation
- the sword of the Spirit which is the word of God

Okay, that's how we become strong, but how do we put on that armor? Note that God doesn't put the armor on us... we do that, but he does provide the mechanism for acquiring the armor.

Ephesians 4:1–6:9 describes in great detail the "walk" of a Christian, so that he can acquire truth, become righteous, proclaim the gospel of peace, build strong faith, be saved, and learn to accurately wield the word of God.

Don't expect God just to pour all those attributes on you... they have to be developed by conquering sin in our lives, learning humility in the service of others, the continual study of God's word, and sallying forth to meet and conquer our enemies who are the "principalities, the powers, the world rulers of darkness and against the spiritual hosts of wickedness in the heavenly places."

Don't think you can do that by yourselves. Discipline yourselves to be completely armored soldiers of Christ in an army waging war with Satan!

Shepherds and Sheep

One of the ways God describes his people is as a flock of sheep... not as a gaggle of geese or a herd of cattle for instance.

The human/animal bond between sheep and a shepherd is very advanced. The sheep are dependent upon humans... much more so than geese or cattle would be.

The sheep's best method of defense is to "flock" together... to circle up and depend upon each other for defense. Of course, the best defense for sheep is a caring shepherd.

Sheep have economic value to the shepherd. The shepherd doesn't just have sheep because he likes sheep. Their wool can be gathered to make fabric, they provide milk which can be converted to cheese and butter, and, of course, they provide meat.

The church is compared to a flock of sheep because of their dependency upon the great shepherd Jesus Christ and also because of their dependency on the human shepherds of a local congregation/church.

Christians, like sheep, depend upon each other for their defense against Satan and his agents and, of course, depend upon their shepherds for defense.

Christians, like sheep, have an economic value to their owner. God doesn't just have Christians around because he likes Christians. Christians have a spiritual economic value to him. In Ephesians 2:8–10, God saves us by his grace, (the free gift of Jesus Christ), but we were created (in a relationship with Jesus Christ) to perform good works.

God provides shepherds to his flock so they can be spiritually nourished through his word. That spiritual nourishment builds faith, and faithful Christians, in turn, live sacrificial lives through the performing of good works for the benefit of other Christians and the world.

In this New Year, work hard to attend every service you possibly can, because in that "flocking" together we build relationships and find opportunities to serve each other. Get involved with the congregation. We grow together by shared experiences. Cast fear and doubt away, and remember what Jesus told his disciples . . . if you just had a little bit of faith, you could move mountains.

Let's move a few mountains in this upcoming New Year.

Jesus and the Two Thieves (Luke 23)

Jesus was, of course, crucified between two thieves... one on his right, and one on his left. They not only suffered the same brutality as Jesus suffered, but also witnessed all the emotional abuse he suffered.

The Rulers "scoffed" at Jesus. The word "scoff" means literally to "hold the nose up"... to sneer and to show contempt.

The Soldiers "mocked" Jesus. The word "mock" literally means to make sport or to jest.

One of the thieves, after witnessing this, joined in and "railed" at Jesus. The word "rail" means to literally blaspheme which is "speech defamatory of divine majesty." A sin punishable by eternal death.

The other thief didn't join in with the crowd. He had witnessed all the things the first thief witnessed and had witnessed what his fellow thief said and "rebuked" him for it. He stood up for Jesus.

It's never wrong to stand up for Jesus or to stand up for anyone else being abused wrongly. The thief was guilty of being a thief and accepted his punishment for that crime, but he was smart enough to know that the door to eternity was about to open for him and the one hanging on the cross next to him held the keys to that door.

In Matthew 20, the mother of James and John asked that her two sons be permitted to sit at the right and left of Jesus when he became a King. Jesus replied that was not his honor to give.

I guess that if you can't be honored by sitting on the right or left side of Jesus in his Kingdom... it might be very honorable to be on his right or his left when he was crucified.

One thief is in Heaven right now wearing that honor. The other thief is in Hell lamenting his foolish mistake of blaspheming God as he hung on a cross. Be careful not to scoff, mock, or rail (by speech or by action) at Jesus. It could be a fatal mistake.

Influence

In Larry White's class tonight, we talked about influence and all the ways we can enhance that. As Christians, we are changing spiritually into Jesus Christ and, as Christ is formed in us, we become powerful influencers without even trying that hard.

Let me give you a few examples. Many years ago, several Parkway members got together to play volleyball along with whoever else wanted to play. James was one of those other guys... about my age and looked like he had tried about everything this life has to offer. One evening, he called me to the side and asked me to pray for him and his wife... they were having problems. That was the opening I was looking for and we prayed, but I also invited him into our home. He started attending with us and. at some point, he told me he hadn't been to church since he was a kid. but saw something in our lives that was lacking in his and wanted to make a change.

The other guy was also a volleyball player. He had been a drug dealer and been shot a few times and spent some time in prison. Also, he told me he had been with about a thousand women. I asked him how that happened, and he said that when the women came to buy drugs you also usually had sex with them. Of course, all that was in the past for him. Anyway, he was a really nice guy and I liked him. At some point, he started going to the church where he was raised, got married and was very active in his congregation. He was a contractor, and we hired him to do a few little jobs at the congregation where he also became friends with David Smitherman.

At some point, he told me that the reason he started going back to church was because of me and David Smitherman and his respect for us. I had no idea.

I see people putting bumper stickers on their cars about Jesus and getting religious tattoos and quoting Bible verses at the drop of a hat, and all that is OK... but let me see it in your lives, because that's the greatest advertisement there is for Jesus Christ. You want to be of great influence? Transform into Jesus Christ and be active in the community where people can see Him, and you will help change a few lives.

Memories and Parts

One of the things I recognize about myself is that I have a short memory, and I've come to realize that a short memory is both a blessing and a curse. It's a blessing because, generally, I don't remember the wrongs people have done to me, and it's a curse because, generally, I don't remember the good either. As my wife says, every day is a brand new day for me.

I know people who are just the opposite... they remember everything bad and good. I guess that's a blessing and a curse, too.

I read a psychology book the other day where a psychologist made a diagnosis that his patient suffered from "memories." The patient couldn't let go of the horrible things that had happened to them, and those memories caused both an emotional and a physical affect upon them.

One thing God's word tells us is that he can cleanse our consciences for us, and he provides several mechanisms to achieve that. I'm not saying that it's easy or that it happens overnight, but I believe everything that God says and believe that he's a great healer.

I guess the best way to be is to have a short memory of the bad things folks have done to us, and a long memory about the good things they've done for us. I've got a feeling that God has forgotten all my shortcomings and treasures the good things I have done. Oh, to be like him.

We've all got parts. God has his part, and we have our part. Take a look in the scriptures and learn your part and all will be... well with you.

Imagine Two Families

Imagine two families.

The first family has parents who never discipline their children. Oh, they may voice displeasure and even disappointment in their children's behavior, but they love their children so much that they cannot bring themselves to discipline them.

The second family is exactly the opposite. The parents are constantly watching their children, looking for any opportunity to discipline them.

Most people can clearly see that these are two extremes of parenting and neither serve the best interests of the children. What cannot be clearly seen is while we may reject these extremes of parenting our children, many of us accept these extremes when they are applied to how God interacts with his children.

Take, for instance, those who are so assured of their salvation that they live however they want to—confident that like the doting parents, God loves them so much that he overlooks anything and everything they do.

Conversely, there are those who are so worried about committing a single sin and possibly losing their salvation and, because of it, they are crippled with fear.

Like the two extremes of parenting, the extreme views of how God deals with his children are incorrect as well.

Most of us can see that effective parents both reward and punish their children in an atmosphere of love, understanding that kids will make mistakes, but they are still our children. There may be a point in families where children totally reject their parents and live evil lives.

As parents, we cannot accept that, but we are always looking for these wayward children to realize their mistakes and return to us. We are looking and praying for the chance to forgive them.

I think this middle ground best portrays how God deals with his children. Study the scriptures and watch how Jesus interacted with Peter for a fuller understanding of this.

It Takes a Village

On the subject of child rearing, adults (other than parents) can have a major impact on the development of children. It seems to me that a lot of adults treat kids as if they are either non-existent or minor irritants. Better to be ignored than interacted with.

I love kids, I like joking around with them, picking on them and throwing the football with them after church. It is no coincidence that kids like me. Some have said that "Rob is just a big kid." OK, I'll take that.

I had a client in the other day who mentioned to me that her adult son commented that his time cleaning cages at Tejas with Walker were some of the most memorable that he had experienced. Interesting… I'm sure Walker doesn't feel that way.

When Lauren was little, I took her on a farm call and pulled a calf. The rancher named the calf "Lauren" and she's never forgotten that.

When clients bring their kids into the clinic, I always shake their hands and introduce myself to them and ask them things like: What did you get for Christmas? Are you ready for school? What are you going to be for Halloween? And the like.

I ask them to help me lift their dog up on the table. There's nothing funnier than a five-year-old kid trying to pick up an 80-pound dog. Before I vaccinate their dogs, I give them a dog treat and tell them to reward their pet after I give the shots. I ask them if they want a shot or if they want their ears checked. If I have time, I take them back to the kennel and let them see all the animals.

I give kids empty syringes so they can practice being Veterinarians at home.

Sometimes at church, I'll give things to the kids. I might buy a bunch of fossilized shark teeth on eBay and give them each a shark's tooth.

Brandon, my nine-year-old "little brother" in the Big Brother/Big Sister program spends a lot of his time during the summer hanging out at the clinic with me. I've taught him to introduce himself, walk up to a client, look them in the eye, and shake their hands. Also, when they ask him how he's doing to respond in kind. Brandon can give a dog a shot and do lots of things around here.

Create some memories; teach these kids a thing or two... they will grow up one day.

Note this verse from Deuteronomy 8:5...

> "Know then in your heart that as a man disciplines his son, so the LORD your God disciplines you."

It is not in the best interests of a child for a parent to give them too much. Many think it is a parent's obligation to give a child the best of everything... not true.

For example, in the Calallen High School parking lot, I see a lot of nice new cars that the students are driving.

In 1970, when I was 16 years old, I bought my first car with the money I earned throwing newspapers. It was a 1965 Pontiac Lemans and it cost me $400. Dad didn't help me.

Fast forward to 1998, I told Walker and Lauren that I would help buy them a car. Whatever money they saved up I would match. Walker saved $400 and we bought him a car that cost $800. Lauren saved $3000 and we bought her a car that cost $6,000.

Lauren later bought a new car and sold her old car to Walker... he is still driving it.

God didn't give Israel everything they wanted during the 40-year wilderness wandering, he gave them just what they needed and no more to teach them humility. He used that lesson to teach future generations a sense of appreciation and thankfulness for a time when he would give them more than they needed.

Teach your kids humility when they are young, and when they grow up and are the type of people they need to be... give them plenty.

That's what God did with his children.

Admonishment and King David

One of the responsibilities Christians have for each other is admonition. That's a Bible word for correcting improper or sinful behavior. It is really an act of love. Its purpose is to help keep each other on the straight and narrow so we can all go to Heaven.

But it's a ticklish subject. I mean, who likes to be corrected by others... right? Done properly, it can have great results but done improperly it can be a disaster. So, it needs to be thought out and prayed about.

First of all, I think you have to earn the right to admonish someone else. In my opinion, that means you must have some type of positive relationship with the person. They need to know you care about them and have their best interests at heart.

I might need to admonish someone I barely know, but its better coming from someone else who has "earned" the right. I have seen folks who needed to be admonished and have identified someone who was close to that person and asked them to help out. It turned out well.

Admonishment is a bit of an art as well. Consider the case of Nathan and David. David needed to be admonished, but he was a King, and usually people in power aren't great at taking advice. Nathan devised a story about a great villain and waited for David's reaction and then Nathan told David that he was the villain.

David had judged himself.

If you could pick anyone in your home congregation to admonish you, who would it be? For me, it would be an older person who has a humble disposition, someone who is reticent about things like that. Not someone who took joy or smug satisfaction in the process. Someone like my mother maybe.

Failure to admonish others is really selfish and unloving. It's like first aid for a bleeding wound... it needs to be bandaged. Don't just watch someone "bleeding out" and fail to act. Step up... you might just save someone and yourself along the way.

Parable of the Three Shepherds

A successful sheep rancher called his three Shepherds together and assigned them 100 sheep each. He sent them out into the countryside to pasture their sheep with instructions to report back in a year.

The first Shepherd found forage for his sheep, cared for the occasional illness or injury that came up, protected them from predators, and when the occasional sheep got lost, he searched diligently until he found it... dead or alive. He loved his sheep.

The second Shepherd behaved in a similar fashion except that when one of his sheep strayed off, he would make a cursory sweep for it and call for it by name, but if it failed to show up, he figured he had made the effort and went back to tending the rest of the sheep and soon forgot about the lost sheep.

The third Shepherd found pasture for his sheep but was kind of a "hands off" guy. The sheep needed to learn to tend for themselves and be responsible for themselves. If a sheep strayed off, he didn't look for it. He figured if the sheep didn't appreciate the benefits of the flock, then it could do what it wanted. If it came back... fine, but if it stayed away... fine.

At the end of the year the Shepherds returned for an accounting of their flocks. The first Shepherds sheep were in good shape and the Ewes had all "lambed" and the flock had increased to 175 sheep. He had lost a few sheep due to predation and health related issues, but all in all, he had done a good job and managed everything under his control.

The second Shepherds flock tallied in at 143 head of sheep.

The third Shepherd's flock had decreased in size to 88 head of sheep due to his faulty philosophy of individual responsibility and a "hands off" approach. The Sheep Rancher fired the third Shepherd for losing so many sheep due to his negligence.

The Sheep Rancher is Jesus. The Shepherds are his appointed Elders/Bishops. The sheep are the church. The roundup and tally are the Judgment Day.

Ask a Simple Question

Julie pointed out something about me the other day. She said I like to make conversation with ordinary people, like wait staff at a restaurant, or workers that come to our house, or bus drivers, or cruise ship staff. I guess she's right... who am I to argue with her? Invariably though, I will ask those kinds of folks this question..."Where do you go to church?" What I'm looking for is those who are not going anywhere or those who are not happy where they are going. Whereupon, I have Julie give them a Parkway Church of Christ business card.

I've had some success with that. I had a waitress tell me that she had been struggling and thought I was sent from God. A guy came out the other day to do electrical work at our home and he said he and his young family would be attending. But who really knows how much success there has been? Sometimes, you just can't tell.

I am friends on Facebook with a concierge who worked at a hotel we stayed at in Italy. I'm also friends on Facebook with a young Filipino guy who worked on a cruise ship we were on. Also, a Russian tour guide. Of course, on Facebook I'm not ashamed of my faith and they see the religious articles I occasionally share.

Work at being friendly with everyone and don't be afraid to ask the simple question..."Where do you go to church?" Maybe, just maybe, you were sent from God to help someone discover their faith.

Spiritually Board Certified

A renowned and famous board-certified veterinary internist once made the comment during a lecture that any veterinarian who picked a subject, kidney disease for instance, and read up on that subject for 20 minutes every day would become an expert on that subject.

I suppose that's good advice for any kind of occupation or for any kind of hobby.

What about for the Christian? What if a Christian picked a book/epistle or any Bible subject and studied on it for 20 minutes every day? What if, like the internist, the Christian reviewed any new information written by experts that might come out? What if the Christian, like many veterinarians, joined a chat group to discuss the subject of interest with other Christians?

That Christian could conceivably become an "expert" and could become a valuable resource to his local congregation and other congregations, and maybe the world. He might publish his works. He might lecture.

What if in a congregation several members each chose a different subject and became experts? What would that congregation look like?

What are we waiting for to achieve something that great and that only costs 20 minutes a day? The five-talent man would probably spend 40 minutes a day.

David the Shepherd Boy Who Would Become King

From his youth, David shepherded his father's flocks of sheep. In all probability, he carried his camping equipment on a cart. He would build his own fire and cook his own meals and clean up after himself. His dad would send him supplies from time to time. Shepherds might spend months to years away from towns and town life.

During the day, he watched the sheep graze all day long and cared for all their needs. Undoubtedly, he helped the ewes deliver their lambs, helped clean them up, assisted them in learning how to nurse, and whatever else they needed.

During his free time, he became expert with a sling and could kill (with a stone) an eagle that might prey upon a baby lamb. Those sling-propelled stones could also fend off and kill larger predators like wolves, coyotes, lions, etc.

David, in his hours of being alone, also learned to play musical instruments and composed songs. Those songs were sung to his audience of sheep to calm them down when needed. David also spent a lot of time looking at nature and contemplating God... praying and singing songs of praise to him.

David learned to be Shepherd of Israel by shepherding sheep. He understood about taking care of God's flock of people and seeing to their needs. He killed the Philistine giant, Goliath, who was threatening God's flock, Israel, with a sling-propelled rock to the head, just like he had done many times before when predators threatened his sheep.

David sang to his people about God and wrote poetry about the God he had learned about while tending sheep. Nature is a great teacher.

When David was off in those far away pastures grazing sheep, he had no idea he would one day be King of Israel (and no one else did either), but God knew. You may think you have the smallest and most insignificant job in the world, but set your eyes and the course of your life on God, because God can do great things with humble people.

Good Times in Heaven

I was talking to my high school Bible class the other day and I asked them what they thought Heaven might be like? I didn't get much of a response.

When I read descriptions of Heaven, it's like streets of gold, gates of pearl, and walls of precious stones. Plus... activities like worship and singing before the throne of God. For me, I can't get too excited about walking on a street paved with gold and, although I like to sing, after a while I get tired of singing. Plus... I know some people who don't even like to sing.

I asked my class... what would be the perfect Heaven for you? What would you like to be doing up there?

One said... I would play my guitar every day. Others talked about playing video games all day long. I guess for me it would be playing Volleyball or eating great food or laughing or spending time with loved ones.

Here's the thing... a lot of those descriptions about Heaven in the scriptures are figurative... not literal.

God uses figurative descriptions to describe immeasurable value in timeless terms that humans can understand.

I told my class that all those fun things we like to do now and the enjoyment those things bring us... that whatever God has planned for us in Heaven... it will be 1000 times funner... maybe a million times.

Have faith in God that he knows how to reward his children. The good things of earth are merely a foreshadowing of those things that God is going to surprise us with in Heaven

Faith is Like a Seed

> "The kingdom of heaven is like a mustard seed, which a man took and planted in his field. Though it is the smallest of all seeds, yet when it grows, it is the largest of garden plants and becomes a tree, so that the birds come and perch in its branches" (Matthew 13:31).

I don't know much about mustard seeds, but I do know about acorns and oak trees. Imagine you found an acorn and didn't know quite what it was. Oh, you knew it was some kind of seed but didn't know what the seed would produce so you planted it beside a creek. Time goes by and some sixty years later you visit that creek again and lo and behold there is a grand old oak tree. An oak with a big old trunk and massive branches that spread so far that it seemed like it would take three days just to walk around it.

You notice that all kinds of birds are roosting in it. Squirrels gather the acorns and deer eat what's left on the ground. During the heat of the day the cattle find rest under its shade. Travelers rest under the tree and camp at night. You're amazed at what that little acorn had become and how it had blessed the rest of nature.

Jesus didn't speak this parable to teach people about growing trees. He taught it to show what the seed of Faith can do in our lives. Faith in Jesus Christ is like that acorn. You might not have a real clear idea of what it will grow into when it's planted in your heart, but given time, you're likely to be amazed at how it can change your life...and the lives of others.

Imagine being married to a godly wife and raising children who love and respect you. Imagine what it would be like if everyone around liked and respected you. Imagine what it would be like if God chose to bless you with all the good things life has to offer, all because He loves you as an obedient and faithful son. And, lastly, imagine what it would be like if the day you died, everyone gathered to pay their respects to you and the building wouldn't hold them all. And your children and your grandchildren cried their eyes out because they wouldn't be able to see your gentle and loving face again this side of heaven.

You might give some thought to how you want to live and die in this life and consider planting that seed in your heart. Give it a little water from time to time and do some weeding around it and above all... trust in God. And get ready for God to amaze you.

Expressions of Joy and Condemnation

> And David danced before the LORD with all his might, wearing a priestly garment. So David and all the people of Israel brought up the Ark of the LORD with shouts of joy and the blowing of rams 'horns. As the ark of the covenant of the LORD was entering the City of David, Michal daughter of Saul watched from a window. And when she saw King David dancing and celebrating, she despised him in her heart (2 Samuel 6:14–16).
>
> When David returned home to bless his own family, Michal, the daughter of Saul, came out to meet him. She said in disgust, "How distinguished the king of Israel looked today, shamelessly exposing himself to the servant girls like any vulgar person might do!" (2 Samuel 6:20–21).

The event recorded above illustrates King David's and the people's great joy at the return of the Ark of the Covenant. There was singing and music, and David, perhaps overwhelmed with great joy, danced in celebration. It was a big event!

However, David's wife, Michal, wasn't too impressed with David's behavior and dressed him down good. She was disgusted with him and mocked him, saying he was "vulgar."

David defended himself and told Michal… God chose me over your precious father, Saul, and he did it for a reason. You may not like it, Michal, but I serve God and I will celebrate before him, and if you think my behavior was undignified, just wait… I will become more undignified in my celebration of Him. Yay David!

We kind of see the same thing today… people's expression of joy before the Lord. I've seen people lifting their arms up and swaying with the singing. I've seen clapping and whooping and hollering. Even people speaking during a public prayer, saying things like… "amen" and "tell it brother."

I'm uncomfortable with that kind of thing because that's not my culture. I was raised to sit in the pew and keep my mouth shut and my arms down, but to tell you the truth I kind of wish I was free to express my joy like David expressed his.

Just because I'm uncomfortable with expressive behavior, it doesn't make that behavior wrong, and I'd better think two or three times before I condemn others for it.

Michal was the daughter of a king who wasn't like her husband-king, and, in her princess pride, she failed to account for the fact that she married a king who was really just a shepherd boy at heart, and whom God loved very much. She should have gone down and danced in joy with him.

Way too bad for her that God cursed her so she would never bear God's anointed son, David, a son...and never have a chance to be named in the lineage of Jesus Christ. Huge mistake... gigantic.

Joseph, Daniel, Esther/Mordecai: Forerunners of...

There's a common motif that is repeated throughout the Bible... a person of faith (man or woman) with humble beginnings rises to great heights being blessed by God and those blessings extend to the people around that person.

Let's look at three examples... Joseph, Daniel, and Esther/Mordecai.

Joseph, of course, was hated by his brothers and sold into slavery. He excelled as a slave and ascended to second in command of the nation of Egypt (behind only Pharaoh). Joseph was a Jew, and the Egyptians despised Jews and would not even eat with them. God blessed Joseph and, as a result, Pharaoh and the nation of Egypt were also blessed.

Daniel, as a young Jew of noble birth, was taken into the Babylonian captivity and made to serve in the court of King Nebuchadnezzar. After many challenges (that Daniel overcomes with his faith) he is made...

"Ruler over the entire province of Babylon and placed in charge of all its wise men." God blessed Daniel, and the nation of Babylon was also blessed.

Esther and her father-figure Mordecai are Jews in the Medo-Persian Empire. The queen of the empire has been demoted and a new queen is being sought. Esther is one of 127 beautiful women competing for that honor and the young Jewish maiden is selected. She is wife and queen to the most powerful King of the world. Mordecai is also elevated to the number two political position of the empire. Esther and Mordecai overcame trials of racism and threats of death to reach their positions.

God's blessings extended to the Medo-Persian Empire because of Esther and Mordecai.

Let's re-examine the motif... humble beginnings, faith, God blesses the faithful and the nations they are associated with. Note that, in these three examples, non-Jewish nations are blessed. Nothing recorded in the Bible is accidental or just serves for entertainment value.

Consider Jesus Christ... humble beginnings, no formal education, he is persecuted for his faith and teachings... even to death, but arises to sit at the right hand side of Jehovah God, and all nations are blessed... Jew and Gentile... past, present, and future.

All these stories in the Bible lead us to Jesus Christ and give us great confidence that no matter what our position in life is, no matter how we are mistreated no matter... anything. Maintain and cultivate your faith and God will bless you, too, and... maybe, just maybe, bless your family, your city, your state, and your nation.

The Lost Sheep: Eating with the Wrong People

One of the things Jesus was criticized for was eating and associating with sinners (Mark 15:2). Jesus answered that criticism by telling the story of a sheep herder who had 100 sheep. One of the sheep wandered off and the shepherd searched for it and, when he found it, he was so happy that he called all his friends to share the good news with them.

He concludes the story by stating, "I say this unto you, that even so, there shall be joy in heaven over one sinner that repents, than over 99 righteous persons who need no repentance."

Don't get the wrong idea about Jesus; he didn't eat and associate with sinners just because he liked to hang out with them and appreciated their company.

Whenever Jesus was around sin, he addressed the sin.

He had a purpose; he was trying to get sinners to repent and lead righteous lives. They couldn't repent unless they felt guilt for their sins. They couldn't feel guilt for their sins unless someone made them feel guilty.

Also, don't get the wrong idea about God... he likes righteous people, but he gets real happy when a sinner turns from his sin and becomes righteous.

I'll tell you, I feel the most comfortable when I am around righteous people. They are my favorite kind of people to be around. But you know what? There's not going to be much "joy in heaven" if Christians just hang out with each other. We've got to put ourselves in a position to have influence over sinners, because if we can turn them, the folks up in heaven are going to be real happy. Go look for those lost sheep... they're out there.

Eating with the Worst

> Then Levi held a great banquet for Jesus at his house, and a large crowd of tax collectors and others were eating with them. But the Pharisees and the teachers of the law who belonged to their sect complained to his disciples, "Why do you eat and drink with tax collectors and sinners?" Jesus answered them, "It is not the healthy who need a doctor, but the sick. I have not come to call the righteous, but sinners to repentance." (Luke 5:29–32).

In this text, Jesus is dining with some of the worst outcasts of Jewish society and, when questioned, he describes himself as a doctor who is healing the sick.

Just to follow up on that... what kind of medicine was Dr. Jesus using?

The text does not indicate he was doing any teaching or identification of sin with accompanying admonition. No, Jesus was socializing with these spiritually sick people. Undoubtably, he was going to follow up with some of those tactics, but he started by sharing a meal and getting to know them.

What kind of social outcasts might we share a meal with today? Drunks and drug abusers? Prostitutes? Homosexuals?

I recall several years ago a young man came to the building asking for money to buy a meal at Whataburger. I asked him why he wasn't working. Somewhere along the way I found out that he had been living with his girlfriend in her parents' home and the father had kicked him out. I told him the father should never have allowed him in the house in the first place and he deserved to be kicked out. I was pretty proud of that answer.

In retrospect, and especially when considering these verses, I wish I had taken him to Whataburger and shared a meal with him. I'm guessing that's what Jesus would have done, and who knows what might have happened? O' to be like him!

Events from God: Local, City-wide, and the Whole Earth

When Jesus was born, God sent an angel to some shepherds to inform them of what happened. Other angels and the "Heavenly host" appeared and, with their voices, praised God. He also sent a star that could be seen from the east so that wise men could follow it to find Jesus, and when they found him, they identified him as the "King of the Jews," and they worshipped that little baby Jesus.

When Jesus was crucified, God put out the sun so that all was in darkness. God also caused an earthquake, rocks were split open, and many of God's holy people who had died became alive again and walked out of their tombs.

The things that God did at the birth of Jesus were different than the things he did at the death of His Son. The things God did in the small town of Bethlehem were smaller, and to a select group, than the things he did in the capital city of Jerusalem, where everyone in the city could see what was happening.

When Jesus comes in his glory, it will be on an even more massive scale... not just small groups of people like at his birth or even a whole city like Jerusalem at his death.

Jesus will descend from Heaven on the clouds with his mighty angels, and every eye on the earth will be able to see him. There will be noise..."a cry of command," "voices of the arch angels," and "the sound of the trumpet of God." There will also be a great "wailing from all the tribes of the earth."

And, at his judgment, "the heavenly bodies will be burned up and dissolved, and the earth and the works that are done on it will be exposed."

The first two miraculous events have already occurred and were seen by witnesses to be written about for our benefit. Let me suggest that the third promised event will be just as real.

Don't be among all the "wailing tribes of the earth." Be saved from that wondrous and terrible event by believing in Jesus and by being washed in his blood so that you can be among all the rejoicing tribes of the earth gathered around the throne of God.

Hearing and the Parable of the Sower and the Seed

Most of us are familiar with the account of the Parable of the Sower and the Seed in Luke 8.

The seed is the word of God and it's planted in different kinds of hearts... the "wayside" where Satan snatches the word out of their hearts before it can even grow a root. The "rocky soil" where the word takes root, but before faith can grow, they are tempted and fall away. The "thorny soil" where the word is choked out by things that compete for our time and the good "rich soil" where the word develops a deep root and is very productive.

The primary application of this parable is not to the planter of God's word... it is to the hearer of God's word.

Note that Jesus' explanation transitions from the agricultural side to a description of a lamp and light and the need to let it shine. The words "hear" and "heard" occurs six times in the parable, and the explanation of the parable and then culminates with the light/lamp explanation with the words "Take heed therefore how you hear..."

You can be a "wayside" hearer, a "rocky soil" hearer, a "weed choked" hearer, or a "good soil" hearer.

You are in control of how you hear God's Word... Jesus said so.

And then, at the close of this explanation, Jesus' mom and brothers come looking for him and Jesus, addressing the crowd, said to them, those who "hear the word of God and do it" are my mother and brothers.

Those who hear and do are those who believe and shine. If you do that, you will be productive.

How to Find Lost Sheep

The context of Matthew 18 begins with a question from Jesus' disciples... "Who is the greatest in the Kingdom of Heaven?"

Jesus answers by talking about humility, receiving "little ones," and not causing them to stumble.

He continues by asking them if they had 100 sheep, and 1 of them strayed, wouldn't they leave the 99 to go find the lost 1?

He concludes that story with the statement..."even so, it is not the will of God that one of these 'little ones' should perish."

Here are some questions that should be asked... Who is the owner of the sheep? Who are the 99 sheep? Who is the lost sheep, and how do we find and bring the lost sheep back? I think those questions are answered in verses 15–17.

- Matthew 18:15a: "If your brother sins (or sins against you), go and show him his fault."

The lost sheep is the sinner who is also a "little one." His fault, or sin, makes him lost.

- Matthew 18:15b: "If he hears you, you have gained your brother back."

In this story, the one looking for the sheep is his spiritual brother. He takes "ownership" of the other sheep by caring for their safety.

- Matthew 18:16: "If he won't listen, take two or three witnesses, and if he won't hear them, tell it to the congregation."

The congregation are the 99 other sheep who have not strayed.

Here's the thing about the "little ones" who are trapped in the web of sin. We should make every effort to pull them loose. All of us should, not just the Preacher, Elders, or Deacons. We do that by approaching the individual and identifying his sin. If we are rejected, we don't give up. We take a few others with us. If we are rejected, we still don't give up. The whole congregation tries to pull this "little one" out of his sin.

God doesn't want to lose any of his "little ones," and his mechanism for achieving that is the action of the other Christians. Pride and indignation over another's sin is counterproductive.

The Christian arms himself with humility and loving concern to bring the lost sheep back. Sometimes, in spite of all this, the sheep won't come back to the flock. That sheep is no longer part of the flock, and all relationships are severed.

However, remember the prodigal son... that relationship was also severed, but the sheep eventually made his way back.

The greatest ones in the Kingdom are those care and sacrifice for their brother sheep. Be great through sacrifice.

Joseph and Keeping Pure

Joseph was a much-favored slave in the home of Potiphar. He had been bought and paid for, but because God and his blessings were with Joseph… Potiphar recognized Joseph's abilities and elevated him to a level of friendship and partnership.

Somewhere along the way, Potiphar's wife recognized Joseph for other reasons and invited him to have sex with her. It must have come as a surprise to her that Joseph declined. My guess is that Mrs. Potiphar had never been rejected before.

In declining her offer, Joseph tried to reason with her. He explained that her husband had been so good to him that he could not betray him, and even more importantly, could not betray God who had been even better to Joseph than Potiphar had been. But she was beyond reasoning. Every day, she tried to entice him to have sex with her.

Lesser men would sooner or later have sex with her. That's what she wanted, why not give it to her? But Joseph believed in God, and that belief propelled him to resist her and not be in a situation where he was alone with her. He was acting with his brain and not his hormones.

But one day, Mrs. Potiphar set a trap for Joseph. She dismissed all her household servants and waited for Joseph to come in to attend to his duties. No doubt she was dressed in a revealing way and looked good and smelled good. Once more, she grabbed his cloak to prevent him from leaving and begged him to go to bed with her, but Joseph slipped out of his cloak and got away.

Realizing that, despite her best attempts, she would never have sex with Joseph, she made up a story and accused him of attempted rape. If she couldn't get him one way she would get him another way. And so, Joseph went to prison.

I'm convinced that Joseph was no different than any other young man. He liked women and was attracted to what God had created for man, but he also knew there was a line he could not cross.

Joseph is a great example for young men today. There is a class of women today who are very sexually aggressive, whose only desire is to use their charms to achieve sexual victory over God's people and over the spouses of God's people... undoubtedly as agents of Satan.

Don't sin against your body, which is a temple of the Holy Spirit. Don't sin against a husband, and most importantly, don't sin against God who has done so much for us. Use the brains that God gave you and control yourselves.

Lessons from Sheep: Shepherds and Conflict

> And there was strife between the Shepherds of Abram's livestock and the Shepherds of Lot's livestock. … And Abram said to Lot, "Please let there be no trouble between you and me and between my Shepherds and your Shepherds, for we are brothers. Isn't the whole land before you? Please separate from me and take first pick and I will go the opposite direction" (Genesis 13:7–8).

The scriptures suggest that congregations have multiple Shepherds (1 Timothy 3 and Titus 1). Sometimes Shepherds don't see eye to eye on subjects pertaining to the welfare of the congregation. If those disagreements aren't handled properly, and Shepherds become angry with each other and treat each other as enemies, rather than as brothers, then the congregation is harmed.

Abraham communicated with Lot… he didn't ignore the issue. The life blood of a congregation is effective communication. Shepherds should never make any kind of decision affecting the congregation without first consulting the other Shepherds… even if it's something as simple as what color to paint a classroom. That sort of communication, at its simplest and most innocent level, begins forming the basis for trust.

Notice that Abraham, in his wisdom, saw the direction things were headed with Lot and took steps to prevent it before lasting harm was done.

Abraham reminded Lot that they were "brothers." The importance of that relationship cannot be overstated. The basis for every relationship is trust. If a husband and wife don't trust each other, they aren't going to have a very good marriage, and if a congregation's Shepherds don't trust each other, then nothing can be accomplished.

Abraham, in his humility, told his nephew Lot to pick whatever land he wanted, and he would take whatever Lot didn't want. Shepherds in a congregation should subject themselves in humility to each other (when possible). It's hard for a relationship to go sour if a pattern of subjection has been established. When some sort of crisis arises in a congregation, if the Shepherds have complete trust in each other, they can focus all their strength and might in overcoming it instead of being suspicious of motives.

Abraham greatly valued the livestock (wealth) that God had given him. He also valued his relationship with his nephew Lot, whom he called a brother. In his humility, he allowed Lot to take the best pasture lands. Because of his humility, God blessed him with much more wealth.

Shepherds in congregations likewise should value the sheep they have been placed in charge of and they should also value their fellow Shepherds. God blesses humility, subjection, and sacrifice. Remember that the next time some crisis develops in the congregation, in your marriage, and in any other of your relationships.

The Façade of Righteousness

> "As for you, son of man, your people are talking together about you by the walls and at the doors of the houses, saying to each other, 'Come and hear the message that has come from the LORD.'
>
> "My people come to you, as they usually do, and sit before you to hear your words, but they do not put them into practice. Their mouths speak of love, but their hearts are greedy for unjust gain.
>
> "Indeed, to them you are nothing more than one who sings love songs with a beautiful voice and plays an instrument well, for they hear your words but do not put them into practice" (Ezekiel 33:30–32).

These are the words of Jehovah God speaking to his Prophet Ezekiel, and secondarily spoken to us as well.

These words describe godly people who wear well the façade of godliness. They may attend services well.

They may chastise others who do not attend well. They may speak out in class.

They may shout out an Amen when the teacher/preacher makes a good point.

They may sing well with heart felt enthusiasm.

They may be willing to take a bullet for Jesus Christ. All those things look good, but what good are they if… They are unforgiving and unforgetting?

They talk bad about other people behind their backs? They are easily offended?

They don't sacrifice their own needs for the needs of others?

They are judgmental?

They are characterized by anger and inflammatory words?

They are not only willing to take a bullet for Jesus Christ but also willing to shoot a few others with bullets.

Let's hope when the façade of righteousness is stripped off on the judgment day that God finds that we are righteous through and through.

Hear all of God's words and devote yourselves to them 100%

Learned Reverence

> "Be sure to set aside a tenth of all that your fields produce each year. Eat the tithe of your grain, new wine and olive oil, and the firstborn of your herds and flocks in the presence of the Lord your God at the place he will choose as a dwelling for his Name, so that you may learn to revere the Lord your God always" (Deuteronomy 14:22–23).

The Jews were to take 10% of their crops and flocks and eat those things in a feast before God in a place of his choosing. In doing so they would learn to "revere God always."

So, it seems it may not be natural or accidental to give God the reverence he deserves… rather, reverence is a learned behavior, and it is learned by sacrifice…regular sacrifice.

Let me suggest that the first thing we should learn to sacrifice to God is our time. It takes time to assemble with other Christians to worship, and it takes time to kneel and pray. It takes time to study God's word, and it takes time to meditate on His teachings. It also takes time to "love our neighbors as ourselves."

So, I wonder how much time we should sacrifice to God… 10%, like in tithing? If so… what a deal… we have 90% of our time to please ourselves.

Let me suggest something else for your consideration. Do you suppose it could be true that the more you sacrifice, the more you come to revere God? If so, then giving up only 10% of whatever would not lead to very deep reverence, would it?

Here's the thing… when God gave up his son for us, he purchased and owns us…lock, stock, and barrel, and when we believed in him and were baptized into the blood of his son, we recognized and accepted that fact.

Learn to revere God by matching His 100% sacrifice (Jesus Christ) with your own total sacrifice. After all, the only ones who will live with God in eternity are those who have forsaken all to revere Him.

Last Letters

Near the end of the Apostle Peter's life, he sat down and composed a letter to a group of Christians. The letter wasn't about himself or really anything about his life. It was about encouraging them to keep the faith so that they could inherit eternity.

Recently, Julie and I were on an airliner. When we were going through some rough weather, the pilot announced we were low on fuel, and he was going to have to divert to another airport. As we were going through that rough weather, I considered that this might be my last day on earth, so I opened up the messages on my iPhone and started composing my last words to our children.

Peter's last words to his spiritual children were to get busy and be diligent about developing their Christian character. He also warned them about false teachers who might lead them down the wrong path and shipwreck their faith.

He told them not to worry, but to have confidence in God and if they would follow the path he had set out for them, all would be well.

When I was on that airplane, my last words to my children were about how proud their mother and I were of them, and to tell our grandchildren how much we loved them. I told them to do their part in keeping our family strong and cohesive and lastly, I told them to trust in God... to study his word every day and to lead their lives by it.

I'm sure the people Peter wrote these words to were friends of his, and that at his death they remembered his last words to them and treasured them. We should also treasure Peter's last words and hold them dear to our hearts, and not be lazy in our faith, but to get busy. Those are timely words, just like the words of a father to his children.

I hope God blesses each and every one of you.

The Righteous Flourish ...

> The righteous flourish like the palm tree and grow like a cedar in Lebanon. They are planted in the house of the LORD; they flourish in the courts of our God.
>
> They still bear fruit in old age; they are ever full of sap and green, to declare that the LORD is upright; he is my rock, and there is no unrighteousness in him" (Psalm 92:12–15).

This figure describes God's righteous people as trees planted in God's house that are... flourishing... that is, they are growing the best that they can in the perfect environment... God's House and Courts.

They're not like ordinary trees that grow old, weak, diseased, and unproductive. No... these trees defy aging and are, from an empirical standpoint, young and ageless. Their "fruit" is to declare wonderful things about God almighty.

What was true at the time of this writing (the Israel of King David) must also be true in our day and age... the Israel of Jesus Christ.

After all, God's trees today grow in a better environment... the New Covenant established by the shed blood of Jesus Christ. Growth and productivity not restrained by impossible "Law keeping," but growth and productivity in an environment of "incomprehensible love."

That's why when we look in a mirror, we may see features that demonstrate aging... wrinkles, scars, and deterioration, but what God and fellow Christians see are a stalwart tree that has weathered many storms but come out victorious.

When I look at my aged mother, I don't see her infirmities... I see her life and I stand in awe.

Don't ever give up on God... don't do it. Stay righteous.

Sin: Clarity vs. Confusion

Ephesians 4:17–19 describes the lifestyle of those who had rejected the teachings about Jesus.

- Their thinking was confused.
- Their understanding was clouded.
- They were excluded from the blessings of God because of their ignorance.
- They were hardheaded.
- They became callous and, as a result, engaged in every form of "sensuality" and "impurity."

These are also characteristics of people today. They reject God because they are unwilling to give up their… sexual misconduct, alcoholism, drug use, and other forms of "sensuality" and "impurity."

Even so-called Christians confuse themselves by believing the lie that it is OK to sin every once in a while, and God's grace will cover whatever sins that we might occasionally engage in. God calls for us to hate sin and ruthlessly eliminate it from our lives. We are, in fact, to transform ourselves into the very picture of Jesus Christ.

Don't let our society confuse you about how to live. Look with clarity into God's revealed word and receive all his blessings.

Entering the Promised Land

There are some interesting things that happened to the Israelites after they crossed the Jordan River and before they conquered the city of Jericho (Joshua 5:1–15).

Here are my thoughts.

When God parted the river of Jordan and closed it behind them, there was no going back... even if they wanted to. There was just one path forward, and that was the direction they were headed. One of the first things that God commanded them to do was to circumcise all the males who had not been circumcised over the past 40 years. After this minor surgical procedure, God announces "today I have rolled away the reproach of Egypt from you."

Let me suggest that the "reproach of Egypt" (Joshua 5:9) refers to the Israelites rejection of God when they didn't believe they could conquer the Promised Land 40 years previously. They had rejected God. Therefore, that whole generation of Israelites who had been circumcised in Egypt had to die and a new crop of Israelites who were not born in Egypt but were born in the wilderness had to be raised up. When this new generation was raised up, they were circumcised, not in the wilderness, but on the soil of their promised homeland.

Circumcision was necessary because it was God's mark on them that validated his promise to Abraham that he would give them a land. They were circumcised because he was about to fulfill that promise. Then the Israelites celebrated the Passover. Let me also suggest that this Passover feast had not been celebrated over the past 40 years. So, on the proverbial eve of conquering the first city-state of Jericho, he was reminding them of what He had done to the Egyptians, and the unstated but fully understood message was that he was about to do the same to the Canaanites. The Israelites could not have been celebrating the Passover because they had no unleavened bread... they had been eating manna. The next day God quits sending the manna.

And thus begins the conquest of Canaan. The transitory phase where God sustained the Israelites for 40 years in the wilderness was over. A new generation of Israelites, freshly circumcised, celebrating God's Passover memorial, and fully energized to accomplish God's promise to Abraham stood on the brink of destiny.

Angels from God

There were two times God the Father sent angels to help his Son. Once, after the 40 days of fasting in the wilderness when the Devil had tempted Jesus, and again in the Garden of Gethsemane when Jesus was in distress anticipating the torture he would have to suffer.

These were arguably the two most dramatic and challenging times in the life of Jesus. One was the deprivation of his physical body screaming for the nutrients it needed (that he had denied it), and the other was his emotional anxiety screaming for calm, peace, and self-control in the face of physical torment at the hands of others.

In both cases, God sent angels to administer relief.

2 Peter 2:9 assures us that God knows how to deliver his people out of temptation. That's very reassuring because sometimes our bodies are so wracked with pain and disease that it can affect our behavior towards others, and sometimes we suffer depression, anxiety, and emotional distress which also affects our behavior.

Trust what God said… he knows how to deliver us out of temptation, and he knows the things we suffer from, and he might… just might, send angels to help us. Just like he did with his Son, Jesus Christ.

Don't Believe Every Miracle You See

> "If a prophet or a dreamer of dreams arises among you and gives you a sign or a wonder, and the sign or wonder that he tells you comes to pass, and if he says, 'Let us go after other gods,' which you have not known, 'and let us serve them,' you shall not listen to the words of that prophet or that dreamer of dreams.
>
> For the LORD your God is testing you, to know whether you love the LORD your God with all your heart and with all your soul. You shall walk after the LORD your God and fear him and keep his commandments and obey his voice, and you shall serve him and hold fast to him" (Deuteronomy 13:1–5).

I suppose if we witnessed a miracle today, we would listen pretty closely to what the fellow who performed it had to say. After all, miracles come from God and are designed to get our attention and to validate prophets.

The miracle gets our attention, but then our attention has to shift to what the prophet is telling us, because God occasionally tests our knowledge and devotion to his word. He creates a dilemma. Are we going to believe the miracle, or are we going to believe what he has commanded us in his written word?

The Deuteronomy text says the written word takes priority over miracles. I wonder why? Probably because Satan (and his agents) can work miracles, too, and humans, through trickery, can work pseudo-miracles.

So, as Christians, we can't just expect to be spoon fed God's word. We have to feed ourselves on a regular basis so when God sends a test, we won't fail. This is a test we need to pass... better start studying for it.

Lessons from Coats

Joseph had two coats that were very significant in his life.

The first was a very distinctive coat that his father gave him. His brothers knew their father loved Joseph more than them, and every time they looked at Joseph wearing that coat, they were reminded of it. Finally, they could take no more and sold Joseph to some slave traders and took his beloved coat and doctored it with blood and rents to present it to their father, Jacob. Jacob looked at it and concluded the worst... some wild animal had killed and devoured his beloved son. The second coat was given to him when he served as a slave to the Egyptian, Potiphar. Potiphar's wife made aggressive sexual advances to Joseph and when he was trying to get away, she grabbed his coat to hold him back and he slipped out of it and got out.

Later she told her husband... your Jewish slave raped me, and I cried for help, and he ran away... here is the coat he left. Of course, Potiphar saw the evidence, believed the story and had Joseph thrown in jail.

Note this... both Jacob and Potiphar were presented evidence and a contrived story, and they believed it. They trusted the story tellers and failed to examine their motives.

I personally have been told by believable people that others, whom I also have trusted, have said bad things about me (in confidence). What do you do with information like that?

As for me... I did nothing. In one case, I refused to believe it because I knew the character of the accused individual. In the other case, I accepted that it might be true but decided it wasn't worth pursuing. I didn't let it affect our relationship. I just pretended it never happened and kept being me.

Jacob lost a beloved son (for a period of time), but found him again.

Potiphar lost a servant (forever) who had made him rich, and that servant went on to make the King of Egypt rich.

I guess the lesson of the Two Coats is that you can't believe everything you see, and you can't believe everything you hear. The Two Coats also teaches that there are people out there who are evil schemers trying to separate loved ones.

Carefully consider what you see and what you are told, and who is telling it, so you don't suffer the same kinds of loss.

Early Decisions

I participate (most years) in a Career Day at one of the local High Schools. Of course, I am there to promote veterinary medicine. Along the way, I have told them that they are at a point in their lives where they are going to be making some really momentous and life-changing decisions at a time when they are, perhaps, the least qualified to do so. Things like getting married, furthering their education, freedom to drink alcohol, etc.

Then I tell them that the career they choose can shape them as a person. For instance, as a veterinarian, wherever I go, people want to talk and visit with me and thank me, etc. Why? Because I have helped them with what is sometimes the most precious thing they have... their pets. That kind of continual positive reinforcement has a shaping effect.

On the other hand, there are careers that can be less fulfilling. Consider what it would be like to be a divorce lawyer and day after day see people at their worst. Or a prison guard or working in the tobacco industry. Think how that might negativity shape you.

Another thing to consider is that some careers have a high suicide rate; other careers are hard on families and have a high divorce rate.

Christianity has a shaping effect as well. Leading a good life, a life-long commitment to a spouse, sober living, treating others kindly no matter how they mistreat you has a tremendous shaping effect. As I look back at my life with Julie, I see that many extraordinary blessings have been showered upon us. I can't take credit for any of them... they came from God.

Choose to serve God at an early age, never doubt him and live by faith. He will shape you and bless you, and when you're a little further down the road, you, too, can look back and see that God was with you every step of the way.

Incredible Acts of Heroism

I've been watching re-enactments on Netflix of the heroics of "Medal of Honor" winners. They are very emotional and inspiring. One of the commentators said this:

"Once you cross the line that you are not going to survive anyway, then you are enabled to achieve incredible acts of heroism."

I've heard that sentiment before; they quit fighting for themselves and were just fighting to help their fellow soldiers survive. True sacrificial living on behalf of others.

Christian soldiers have a completely different mindset... I cannot be killed, therefore I'm totally unafraid of what might happen to me (on earth) and am therefore completely free to testify about the Lord Jesus Christ to anyone who will listen.

In fact, that was exactly the mindset of the early Christian martyrs. Today you hear of Christians going into places like North Korea, Iran, China, etc. and you wonder... have they lost their minds? No, they haven't, the bravest soldiers go where they are needed the most and understand that their "Medal of Honor" awaits them in Heaven.

Living Water and God's Garden

We've been in a drought here in South Texas since before January. It's been so dry that we really never had a spring. Of course, you can keep the plants alive with city water, but they really don't thrive. To compound that, in early February, we had a historic freeze that killed a lot of vegetation that wildlife lives on. So, it's been pretty sad around here.

For the past two days we've had rain... four inches of rain at my house. This morning, when I got up and went outside, the White Wing doves were singing their hearts out, and as I checked our plants, they were putting on new growth and leafing out.

That city water has been worked over pretty hard by the water department and is laden with chemicals so it can be safe for our consumption. It can keep plant life alive, but just barely. The water that falls out of the heavens is really what vegetation needs and thrives on... and it's what people need too.

I see congregations that are watered with "city water." The water has been sanitized, chemically treated, bottled up, and labeled by human beings. When congregations are fed this kind of water, they're kind of like plants... stunted and not much growth, collectively or individually,

When congregations are fed the "living" water which comes from Heaven, people are growing spiritually and the congregation is growing collectively, because people would rather live in, and are attracted to, a garden watered from Heaven.

As leaders, let's do our best to provide what the plants in God's garden need... the kind of water they can thrive and grow on. And if we look at our "work" and see that it's stunted and sad, let's take a long look at what we're doing and make whatever corrections we can.

Nourishment in the Lord's Supper

Ephesians 5 states that Jesus cherishes and nourishes the church. Nourishment is necessary for growth.

Ephesians 4 states that we, as Christians, are to grow into the exact image of Jesus Christ.

Jesus nourishes us so we can grow into him and be just like him.

Usually, nourishment means food, so it shouldn't be surprising that Jesus uses food in the Lord's Supper to represent himself, and that, in eating that representation, we turn into him.

Of course, the Lord's Supper is just a figure for what Christians should be literally doing... consuming everything we know about Jesus (as found in the scriptures) and transforming ourselves into him by thinking and behaving just like he did.

When we take the Lord's Supper, we are proclaiming to the world two sacrifices. The sacrifice of Jesus Christ, and the sacrifice of our old selves.

The Lord's Supper should never be just some mundane thing we do by rote, but should be a reminder as we eat the bread and drink the cup that we need to transform ourselves.

Parables...Virgins and Talents

Matthew 24–25 begin with Jesus' prophesying about the destruction of Jerusalem in A.D. 70 with undertones of the Day of Judgement. Then we read of two parables before we get to a section that is definitely talking about the final Judgement Day. In the final Judgement Day, Jesus specifically details the requirements for entering the eternal kingdom. Namely... feeding the hungry, giving drink to the thirsty, taking in strangers, clothing those who need clothes, visiting the sick, and visiting those in prison.

So, now let's look at the parables.

The first one is the parable of the 10 Virgins. They had a job... one job... to carry oil fueled torches to lead the bridegroom into the wedding feast. The problem was that the bridegroom didn't come when they expected. 5 of the Virgins were prepared for that eventuality... they brought extra oil. They got to go into the marriage feast. The others didn't.

The bridegroom is Jesus, the Virgins are Christians, and the wedding feast is Heaven. You have to be prepared when Jesus comes. You have to have enough oil when Jesus comes. The oil is helping the hungry, thirsty, strangers, unclothed, sick, and prisoners. You can't stop engaging in those activities and rest on your laurels, or like with the 5 foolish, the door to the wedding feast will be slammed in your face.

The second parable is about the 5, 2, and 1 talent men. Their master trusted them with money based on their ability, and then came back for an accounting. The 5 and 2 talent men doubled their money and are invited to "enter into the joy" of their Lord.

The one talent man is too lazy to work for the master and returns his investment to him. The master cast the 1 talent man into "outer darkness." Jesus is the master, the servants are Christians. Entering into the masters Joy is Heaven, and being condemned to "outer darkness" is Hell. The investment the master makes in them is the investment Jesus makes in us.

The investment is helping the hungry, thirsty, strangers, unclothed, sick, and prisoners.

To sum it up, Christians need to be continually doing good because they don't know exactly when Jesus is coming. In addition, God has an investment in us that is guaranteed to produce if we will just try. That's all he asks is effort.

Heaven and Hell are waiting. Choose where you want to go by your actions. Don't be lazy.

Story Telling

Jesus was a fellow that liked to tell stories... in fact, you could always count on him for a story. He was also a keen observer on things going on around him, and when he noticed something in particular, he would begin to tell a story.

In Luke 14:7–11, Jesus was at a feast put on by a "Ruler of the Pharisees," which is Jew talk for a really big dog in the Jewish religion. Jesus noticed that the guests were competing with each other for the best seats and, of course, started in with a story.

Here's how it goes... there's a big party and one of the guests decides to sit up by the host, but then another guest came in, perhaps the mayor of the city, and the host tells the guy sitting next to him... "do you mind sitting at the end of the table? I had intended for the mayor to sit here." Jesus concludes that the embarrassment is intense, and it would be better when you came to the party to kind of hang back and let the host sit you in a better place if he chose to.

And then he concludes, "For everyone that exalts himself shall be humbled; and he that humbles himself shall be exalted."

Keep in mind that Jesus tells this story in the middle of the party to guests who had been involved in inappropriate behavior. It does kind of kill the mood at a party.

I like it that Jesus was a storyteller because I like to tell stories, too, but I guess one of the differences between me and Jesus is I usually like to tell stories to entertain people and make them laugh. I've never seen Jesus tell a story just to entertain people.

It's not wrong to bring joy into people's lives... in fact, it's a good thing, but let's also be attentive to what's going on around us, and instead of taking the shortcut of condemning behavior, illustrate it with a story that will stick in the mind of the listener.

That's reminds me of a story. No Joke.

There's an old joke about a farmer who was going broke farming, so he quit and started selling hammers. He would buy hammers for $3 apiece and sell them for $2 each. He was happy and doing pretty good business, but a friend advised him that for every hammer he sold he was losing $1. His reply? "it's more profitable than farming."

That joke is similar to what people sometimes do with their lives. Activities like drunkenness, sexual immorality, unfaithfulness to a spouse, etc. can cause folks to view their lives as being spiritually bankrupt. So, they decide to go to church, pray, or read the Bible every once in a while, without actually correcting the behaviors that got them into such a big mess to begin with.

Going to church, praying, and reading the Bible are good things to do, but until we take some corrective action in our lives and commit ourselves fully to Jesus Christ and his teachings, we are still "going broke"... Like buying hammers for $3 and selling them for $2. Don't make a joke out of your life.

Of Riches, Camels, and Needles

Two rich men are introduced in Luke 18 & 19. One was a Ruler of the Jews who lived according to the 10 commandments, and as such, was well liked and well received in Jewish society. The other was a Jew who collected taxes for the Roman Government. He, on the other hand, was hated because he worked for the enemy. In essence, he was stigmatized and ostracized by his fellow Jews.

The Ruler was living a righteous life and even Jesus recognized that. However, Jesus knew something that the Ruler may not have even known about himself... he loved his money and possessions too much. When Jesus told him to sell it all and distribute the proceeds to the poor, the conversation ended, and the Ruler walked away with great sadness. He loved his money too much.

The Tax Collector, like the Ruler, had heard of Jesus, and when he heard Jesus was in town, he climbed a tree just so he could catch a glimpse of Jesus. He wasn't blind, or crippled, or in need of any miraculous healing from Jesus, he just wanted to see him. And then Jesus did something that violated all the social norms of Jewish society... he noticed the Tax Collector and stayed in his home. You see, the Tax Collector suffered from a non-physical malady... he suffered from a love deficiency.

He had all the money he could want, but no one cared for him.

At Jesus' expression of love, the Tax Collector, Zacchaeus, was overwhelmed and offered something the Jewish Ruler wouldn't give... he offered to give 50% of his possessions to the poor and offered a fourfold restitution to anyone who he might have over charged for taxes.

Jesus' response? "Salvation has come to this house."

The Jewish Ruler asked what he needed to do to be saved. Zacchaeus already knew the answer and with great enthusiasm offered the price.

How does a rich man enter the kingdom of God and how does a camel go through the eye of a needle? By understanding the true value of wealth and using it properly.

Prejudice

Everyone knows what racial prejudice is, but we may not be aware of how old of a problem it is. The scriptures reveal that it was a problem among some very godly people. In Numbers 12:1–15, Moses' sister Miriam and his brother Aaron did not like Moses' wife because she was a "Cushite"... of a different race.

Their prejudice causes them to sin. They "spoke against" Moses by questioning his rank as a prophet... they thought they were just as good as he was. Verse 3 states that Moses was, "very humble, more than any man on the face of the earth."

Miriam and Aaron were not humble... they were the opposite: they were jealous and full of pride.

Cushites were African peoples. In fact, the Septuagint version of the Old Testament calls them Ethiopians. The word Ethiopian is a Greek word that literally means "burnt face."

When God punished Miriam, he gave her the disease of Leprosy. The text says she was turned "as white as snow." It's ironic that Miriam and Aaron disliked Moses' wife because she was a "burnt face" and God punished Miriam by turning her into a shade of white that she didn't want to be.

Prejudice against someone because of their race is a sin of pride. Pride makes us think that we are better than others. Christians are supposed to be humble... counting others as better than ourselves.

Training at the Lord's Supper Table...Hans and Willie

There are several good things about using "waiting on the Lord's Supper table" to train men to serve the congregation.

Let me illustrate that for you. We have a member (Let's call him Hans) who was a little nervous to stand in front of the congregation. However, in talking to Hans, we told him he could be in the outside position and not have to lead a prayer, or read a scripture, or anything else... just pass out trays. He agreed. After a while, I asked him if he would serve at the inside position and say a prayer for the cup. I explained, he wouldn't have to read a scripture or make any comments. He could even write the prayer down and read it. He agreed and did that for a while. Now on his own, he serves on the inside, saying the prayer for the bread, reading scripture, and making meaningful comments.

Training is a process.

Let's use another example (we'll call him Willie). Willie had been a Christian all of his life but was extremely nervous about speaking in front of a large group. His Bible knowledge was excellent. He had a good brain and knew how to use it. He started on the outside... got comfortable and evolved into a great speaker at the Lord's Table. Every time he made comments at the Lord's Table, the congregation's eyes and attention were focused on him... you never heard the same thing twice out of him. In my opinion, Willie was at the top of my list for inspiring the congregation at the Lord's Table.

Hans and Willie were trained to serve the congregation at the Lord's Table. Their talent was discovered, trained, and honed by starting them out small and letting them grow.

"What Then is The Law?"

> What then is the law? It was added because of transgressions, till the seed should come to whom the promise has been made... (Galatians 3:19).

Here's an interesting passage. The referenced Law is the Law given to Moses on Mount Sinai. It was a written Law that regulated almost every aspect of Jewish life. From Adam to Moses, there was no written Law. God communicated to the people either directly or through prophets. From Moses to Jesus, there was the written Law of Moses given on Mount Sinai. From Jesus onward, there was again no written law (on stone or parchment). All communication from God was given through his son... Jesus Christ.

The Galatians passage explains the need for a written Law. It was needed because God was unhappy with the sinful conduct of the people. In addition, it was needed to prepare the people for the coming of Jesus Christ and his superior Law. The Law of Moses micromanaged almost every aspect of Jewish life. The Law of Jesus liberated the Jews and gave them freedom (from the Law) in its simplicity.

With the coming of Jesus, we no longer have a law written on stone or parchments. Christ's law is written on our hearts (2 Corinthians 3:3). The Law that specifically is written on our hearts is to love God and to love our fellow man (Matthew 22:34–40 and John 13:34).

So, then an important question comes up... what is the New Testament? Is it analogous to the Law of Moses?

The answer is no. Christ's Law is written on our hearts. The New Testament is the Christ-authorized and Holy Spirit-inspired writings of the Apostles (primarily) that explains to us the details of how we apply the Law that is written on our hearts. A Law written on our hearts is a law we carry with us each and every day. What a great joy and blessing!

Did You Grow Today?

Tonight, during Bible class, Marc asked us if anyone thought they had grown spiritually today, and I raised my hand.

This morning, there was about 10 minutes left in Bible class, and our security guy tapped me on the shoulder and said someone was in the foyer who wanted to talk to me. I didn't figure it was an emergency, so I told him I would talk to the fellow after class.

When I went back to the foyer, I saw about what I expected to see... a young man who was about 30 years old, tatted up pretty good and looking homeless. When I sat next to him, he didn't smell very pleasant either. As I talked to him, I discovered he was a little different than most... he started sobbing and telling me what a bad life he had lived, and how he didn't know what to do. He had spent some time in jail and had been living on the streets for about 8 months.

He lived by walking up and down streets asking if people needed any help and made a few dollars. He also said some would hire him for a whole day, and then at the end of the day laugh at him and refuse to pay him.

I talked for a while with him, and then Larry talked to him for a while. When services started, he came and sat on the back pew with us and started sobbing. Larry brought a box of tissues to him. Then Noe got up from his seat and sat next to him and consoled him. I made closing announcements, and mentioned a few things about the young man, and the congregation showed an outpouring of love towards him.

I had been wondering what to do with him after services and thought about taking him to lunch with our family, but I was uncomfortable with him being in our car sitting behind us. So, I decided to offer him some money. I looked in my wallet and there were five one-dollar bills and a fifty-dollar bill. I really didn't want to give him the fifty, but the ones were not enough, so I crumpled the 50 in my hand and told him I wanted to help him. Guess what... he refused to take any money. He said he couldn't take any money he hadn't earned. Dude... that is really different... like unheard of. So, I asked him if he would like to go eat lunch with us. He gladly accepted.

We went to a hamburger place, and he only took about two bites out of his hamburger and said his stomach was upset. Later I found out he hadn't eaten in two days.

So... I had been thinking about what to do with him after lunch. I didn't really want to invite him into our home because I still had a notion in the back of my head that this might be some kind of set up. I asked him what he was going to do. He said, walk around and try to make some money and figure out where he was going to sleep tonight.

My conscience whipped up on me again and I said... would you like to spend the day with me? ... yes, he would.

He talked to us about his mom who lives in Fairfield, Texas and I asked him if he would like to use my phone to call her. I heard him tell her that he had been to church and how nice everyone had been to him. She told him that maybe if he came home, they both could go to church.

During the day, he told me he had never been in a church building... that when he was in jail some inmates had shared a Bible with him and he read the Book of Job. He said he was walking down Weber Road, and something told him to turn down a side street and he saw our building and he walked in. He said everyone in the congregation was so friendly to him, and as he sat on the pew and thought about the horrible life he lived, and the unexpected friendliness the congregation had for him, he just started crying.

He said Marc's lesson had a lot of meaning for him. As we were out driving, he had mentioned that he would like to go back home to his mother. I told him that I could find him some odd jobs and if he demonstrated responsibility, I could probably find him a better job or... if he wanted, I would loan him the money to get a bus ticket back to Fairfield. Note... I said I would loan him the money because he had previously rejected free money.

He thought for a minute and said... I would like to go home. Julie got online and bought him a bus ticket for Fairfield, Texas. He leaves at 11:45 tomorrow morning and has a 14-hour bus trip ahead of him. He said with the ticket, the bus company would let him spend the night in the station. Julie, bless her righteous heart, wanted to get him a hotel room, but I told her he was plenty happy with what we had done already.

We went to services with him Sunday night and I was talking to Noe about him, and Noe said... we need to talk to him about being baptized! So, we did.

We baptized Juan right then and right there. When he came out, I was the first one to hug him. He was shaking and sobbing, and held me for a long time, and I cried too.

So, when Marc asked during class if anyone had grown spiritually... yes... definitely me. The Lord took away all my second thoughts and doubts and a soul was saved today.

We have a lot of members with a lot of talents, but thank you Lord for sending Noe to us... he has a great heart!

www.ingramcontent.com/pod-product-compliance
Lightning Source LLC
Chambersburg PA
CBHW061548250926
52052CB00010B/3117

Uncle Rob's Blog

Volume 2